THE MEANING OF LOVE

The Meaning of Love

VLADIMIR SOLOVYOV

Edited
with a substantially revised
Translation
by Thomas R. Beyer, Jr.

Introduction
by Owen Barfield

INNER TRADITIONS  LINDISFARNE PRESS

The translation, substantially revised by Thomas R. Beyer, Jr., for this edition, is based on the original translation by Jane Marshall, published in 1945 by Geoffrey Bles, the Centenary Press, London.

This edition copyright © The Lindisfarne Press, 1985
Introduction copyright © Owen Barfield, 1985

An Inner Traditions/Lindisfarne Press Book

Published by The Lindisfarne Press, P.O. Box 127, West Stockbridge, MA 01266. Distributed to the book trade by Inner Traditions International. All inquiries regarding distribution should be addressed to Inner Traditions International, 377 Park Avenue South, New York, NY 10016-8807.

ISBN 0-89281-068-8

Library of Congress Cataloging-in-Publication Data

Solovyov, Vladimir Sergeyevich, 1853–1900.
    The meaning of love.

    Translation of: Smysl' liubvi.
    1. Love.   I. Beyer, Thomas R.   II. Title.
BD436.S6413   1985   177'.7   85-18037
ISBN 0-89281-068-8 (pbk.)

Printed in Great Britain

INTRODUCTION

INTRODUCTION

The first time I heard the word "sexy" used was in a performance of Bernard Shaw's late play *The Apple Cart*, and I remember the titters it evoked in the audience. It was not long before the neologism had entered into general use; but I think the second World War had intervened before our vocabulary descended even farther to the unlovely, if not positively hideous expression "having sex," ubiquitous now in the media and to be heard even in courts of law. Thus the vulgarization of language reflects, and in doing so helps forward, the decomposition of the human spirit.

The assumption of an emergent evolution, whereby man has merely evolved from the status of an animal, is today built into our language on pretty well all subjects, including notably the subject of sex. It is accordingly taken for granted in most quarters that the sexual instinct is the underlying reality and that what is called 'love' is a late-come embroidery on it. The fact that this word still always denotes sex-love, unless the context otherwise directs, as for instance in its attributive uses—love poems, love tokens, love-sick, love life, etc.—seems at first sight to support this view. The fact that there are nevertheless plenty of contexts in which it means nothing of the sort has led on the one hand to a great deal of confused feeling and confused thinking, and on the other hand to some profound and valuable *distinguos*, one of the latest being C.S. Lewis's *The Four Loves*. It is hardly surprising that not a few have reacted to the confusion by insisting on an opposition amounting to incompatibility between Eros and Agape, between the earthly Aphrodite Pandemos of Plato and his sublime Aphrodite Urania. If they had their way, we should cease using the same word for at least two entirely different things.

That is not the conclusion arrived at by Vladimir Solovyov. Where Lewis, with all due allowance for interaction, divides, Solovyov unites. "For good reason," he writes,

> sexual relations are not merely termed love, but are also generally acknowledged to represent love *par excellence*, being the type and ideal of all other kinds of love (cf. the *Songs of Songs* and the *Apocalypse*).

Others, notably Coventry Patmore, have arrived at the same conclusion on the same or similar grounds, but none I think by the same method. We have to extract Patmore's philosophy of love from poems and aphorisms, whereas Solovyov's approach is quietly scientific. Any attempt, he points out, to account for the sexual relation between human beings and to determine its true function, must account for *all* the phenomena, not only some of them; and yet one very conspicuous phenomenon, left completely out of account in a biologically biased treatment of the subject, is the experience known as being in love.

Not that the other factors are in their turn ignored. Solovyov does not start from the subjective experience of being in love and ingeniously evolve a whole metaphysic from it. He opens with a biological survey, which easily, and to my mind irresistibly, refutes the age-old presumption (based, it would seem, on an unholy alliance between Darwinian theory and a sentence in the Prayer Book marriage service) that the teleology of sexual attraction is the preservation of the species by multiplication. On the contrary, it is apparent from the whole tendency of biological evolution that nature's purpose or goal (or whatever continuity it is that the concept of evolution presupposes) has been the development of more complex and, with that, of more highly individualized and thus more perfect organisms. From the fish to the higher mammals quantity of offspring steadily decreases as subtlety of organic structure increases; reproduction is in inverse proportion to specific *quality*. On the other hand the factor of sexual attraction in bringing about reproduction is in direct proportion. On the next or sociological level he has little difficulty in showing that the same is true of the factor of romantic passion in sexual attraction. Both history and literature show that it

9

contributes nothing towards the production of either more or better offspring, and may often, as in the case of Romeo and Juliet, actually frustrate any such production at all.

Why then has nature, or the evolutionary process, taken the trouble to bring about this obtrusively conspicuous ingredient in the make-up of *homo sapiens*? It is in its answer to this question that the originality (which is not the same thing as novelty) of this little book resides. The answer is approached step by step. It would seem, the argument proceeds, that that ingredient must positively have been an end in itself—and not perhaps an unworthy one. This is a long step already out of the Darwin-Freud paradigm, and one might be not unhappy to rest awhile in it. But it turns out to be only the first step. The next, and the most difficult one, constituting therefore the main substance of the book, is to show that even here nature is after all still at her old tricks, developing quality at the expense of quantity. The rarest complex organization of all, human individuality, *is* an end in itself by contrast with what has gone before; but on a plane now where ends in themselves are also means to an end. It is the plane of what the author calls "the unity-of-the-all idea," or as it was translated in Janet Marshall's earlier English version "the all-one idea."

Being, at the level of human individuality, is characterized above all by a relation between whole and part that is different from the everyday one that is familiar to us. We may catch a glimpse of it if we reflect, in some depth, on the true nature of a great work of art. Recent advocates of 'holism' in philosophy or science seem also to be feeling their way towards it. It is a relation no longer limited by the manacles of space and time, so that interpenetration replaces aggregation; one where the part becomes more specifically and individually a part—and thus *pro tanto* an end in itself—precisely as it comes more and more to contain and represent the Whole.

Sex-love is for most human beings their first, if not their only, concrete experience of the possibility of such an interpenetration with other parts, and thus potentially with the Whole.

> The meaning and worth of love, as a feeling, is that it really forces us, with all our being, to acknowledge for another the same absolute central significance which, because of the power of our egoism, we are conscious of only in ourselves. Love is important not as one of our feelings, but as the transfer of all our interest in life from ourselves to another, as the shifting of the very center of our personal lives.

Love, for Solovyov, is a cross, with both horizontal and vertical co-ordinates. Its horizontal, human, one-one relation is made possible by its other vertical, all-in-one co-ordinate. The light in the shining eyes of an unspoiled boy or girl in love is no merely earthly light. It is a primitive and transient glimpse of the Divine image in another human being, and thus of God's love for man, which is itself the ground of the all-in-unity idea.

> This living ideal of the Divine love, antecedent to our love, contains in itself the secret of the idealization of our love. In it the idealization of the lower being exists together with an incipient realization of the higher, and in this is the truth of love's intense emotion.

Love, our author tells us, is like language. Such significance as the *word* possesses for the formation of human society and culture, *love* also possesses in a still greater degree for the creation of true human individuality. Love is "given," as the meanings of words are given, without our co-operation. But, being given, it demands to be *used*—for the creation of true individuality. The *realization* of "organic solidarity" does require our co-operation. "The task of love consists in *justifying in deed* that meaning of love which at first is given only in feeling"—a doctrine that found early and crude expression in the ideal of chivalry.

I have said that originality is not the same thing as novelty. Originality takes us forward, not because it thinks what was never thought before, but because it thinks in harmony with the 'origin' of its subject matter. Solovyov's "organic solidarity" is no brand-new invention. I see his book rather as a timely and fruitful blossom on a tree, whose roots are deep in the past. The same sap surely was rising in Thomas Traherne's genius when he wrote ·

> That violence whereby sometimes a man doeth upon one creature is but a little spark of that love, even towards all, which lurketh in his nature. When we dote upon the

perfections and beauties of some one creature, we do not love that too much, but other things too little. Never was anything in this world loved too much, but many things have been loved in a false way, and all in too short a measure.

But those roots delve much deeper than the seventeenth century. The tree is perhaps as old as Yggdrasil itself. Only it is not just its roots that are hidden from the eyes of most of us in their fruitful soil. The trunk itself is wrapped around by a mass of historical detritus that had its origin elsewhere and has largely shaped the world in which we live. There are two distinct intellectual genealogies: on the one hand, Bacon-Descartes-Newton-Lyell-Darwin-Freud and the reductionism which has finally succeeded in reducing the humanity of gender to the explicit animalism of 'sex'. On the other—what? Pythagoras-Platonism-Sufism-Dante-the *Fedeli d'Amore* of Renaissance Italy-the Rosa Alchemica-the Rosicrucian impulse-Hermeticism-Romanticism; things we have to dig for rather than having them thrown at our heads. Most significant of all perhaps, if we were to dig assiduously enough, would be the startlingly simultaneous appearance all over Europe in the twelfth and thirteenth centuries of the complex myth of the Holy Grail.

Can we trace any change or development here? Or is it simply the same wisdom-stream surfacing at intervals along its underground course, like the waters in Ruskin's story *The King of the Golden River*? I think we can. I think it will be found that its earlier manifestations—with the exception perhaps of Wolfram von Eschenbach's *Parzifal*—concentrated more on the vertical dimension, on the man-God relation rather than the man-man or man-woman one. Emphasis on the horizontal dimension is of course post-Christian and is still perhaps in its infancy. It is audible in the quotation from Traherne. In Solovyov it is well to the fore.

> "This" may become the "all" only together with others; only together with others can an individual realize his absolute significance—become an inseparable and irreplaceable part of the universal whole, an independent living and original organ of absolute life.

It follows naturally from this that the author should, in his closing pages, touch on the sociological aspects of his doctrine. The relation between the individual and his social or civic unit should be "syzygetic" (from the Greek συζυγια, close union).

> As for sexual love (in the sphere of personal existence), the single "other" is at the same time all, so, on its side, the social *all*, by power of the positive solidarity of all its elements, ought to manifest itself for each of them as a real unity, as the other living being which would fulfil him in a new and wider sphere. . . . This bond between the living human source (personal) and the unity-of-the-all idea incarnated in the social spiritual-physical organism, ought to be a living *syzygetic* relation.

If our social structure is disintegrating, is that not precisely because it has no constitutive spiritual principle, no "idea" in Solovyov's (and Coleridge's) sense of the term, incarnate in it? In the structure that preceded it, namely feudalism, there was such an incarnate idea, the idea of hierarchy; and the true, Dionysian idea of hierarchy is a spiritual principle, involving some measure of interpenetration. It is a mistake to deny its value by looking only at its abuses and its increasing distortion as time went on and accepted hierarchy turned gradually into resentful class-consciousness. But it would equally be a mistake to attempt to restore it. What is needed is a different idea to replace that of hierarchy. And I at least can think of none more suitable, more called for by the *Zeitgeist*, than this of Solovyov's. It is tragic indeed to reflect how few are aware that, as long as sixty years ago, a social structure incarnating the idea of organic solidarity was adumbrated, even into political and economic detail, by Rudolf Steiner in *The Threefold Social Order, World Economy* and other books and lectures.

To revert to my metaphor, there can be little doubt that the continued *life* of human society, if not of the earth itself, will in the long run depend on the life and health of the tree, not on the detritus that is smothering it. We are told that at the age of twelve Solovyov once wrote in a letter to his cousin and one-time fiancée that his idea was the "work of transforming the world." If I can hardly help smiling at this juvenile optimism, neither can I be altogether surprised that he should have felt that way. One might indeed be more inclined to think, in connection with such a far perspective, of other works of his, and notably the apocalyptic *War, Progress and the End of History, Including a Short Story of the Anti-Christ*. And yet I believe it would be difficult to exaggerate the *potential* importance of just this little book about love, because it is a subject with which precisely the young among us are, or ought to be, concerned: What, I wonder, are its actual prospects? I should not like to say. Even in the age that is fast coming upon us we may perhaps assume that there will still be found, here or there, one or two of Chaucer's "yonge fresshe folkes he or she" who have not had all finer sensibility thumped out of them by electronic decibels before reaching the age of puberty; so that what Charles Williams called "the Beatrician moment" never even makes its appearance. Fortunate indeed, if so, will be the bewildered adolescent who finds this golden key in his hands before it is too late, before the dead weight of common sense—*communis sensus*, the shared metaphysic of the society around him—has taught him to abandon the idle fancy of being in love and get down to the serious business of having sex. There will be few enough of them in any case. But then we are told on good authority that "a little leaven leaveneth the whole lump."

Owen Barfield
South Darenth
February 1984

THE MEANING OF LOVE

CHAPTER 1

I

Ordinarily the meaning of sexual love is supposed to lie in the propagation of the species, for which it serves as a means. I consider this view incorrect—not merely on the basis of any theoretical considerations, but above all on the basis of facts of natural history. That propagation of living creatures may take place without sexual love is already clear from the fact that it does take place without division into sexes. A significant portion of organisms both of the vegetable and of the animal kingdom propagates in a non-sexual fashion: by segmentation, budding, spores and grafting. It is true that higher forms of both organic kingdoms propagate by the sexual method, but the organisms which propagate in this fashion, vegetable as well as animal in part, *may* likewise propagate in a non-sexual fashion (grafting in the vegetable world, parthenogenesis in higher insects). Moreover, setting this aside, and recognizing as a general rule that the higher organisms propagate by means of sexual union, we are bound to conclude that this sexual factor is connected not with propagation in general (which may take place also apart from it), but with the propagation of *higher* organisms. Consequently, the meaning of sexual differentiation (and of sexual love) is to be sought not in the idea of the life of the species and its propagation at all, but only in the idea of the higher organism.

We find a striking confirmation of this view in the following important fact: within the limits of animals which propagate exclusively in the sexual mode (the division of vertebrates), the higher we ascend in the hierarchy of organisms, the weaker the power of propagation becomes, but, on the other hand, the greater the power of sexual attraction becomes. In the lowest class of this division—among fish—propagation takes place on an enormous scale: the embryos produced every year by each female are counted in millions; these embryos are fertilized by the male *outside* the body of the female, and the method by which this is done does not admit of the supposition of any powerful sexual impulse. Of all the vertebrate animals this cold-blooded class undoubtedly propagates most of all, and exhibits the passion of love least of all. In the next stage—that of amphibians and reptiles—the power of propagation is far less significant than among fish (though some of the species of this class, not without basis, are assigned in the Bible to the number of creatures that swarm in great quantities[1]); together with a smaller rate of propagation, we already

find in these animals more intimate sexual relations. . . .
Among birds the power of propagation is far weaker, not
only in comparison with fishes, but also in comparison,
for instance, with frogs, yet the sexual attraction and the
mutual attachment between male and female attain a
development unheard of in the two lower classes.
Among mammals—which are already viviparous—the
power of propagation is significantly weaker than
among birds, and sexual attraction, among the majority
at any rate, is less constant; but, to balance that, it is far
more intense. Lastly, in humans, in comparison with the
whole animal kingdom, propagation is effected on the
smallest scale, but sexual love attains its utmost significance and its highest power, uniting in the superlative
degree, both constancy in the relation (as in birds) and
intensity of passion (as in mammals). So then, sexual
love and propagation of the species are found to be *in
inverse ratio* to each other: the more powerful the one,
the weaker the other. Speaking generally about the aspect which is being examined, the whole animal kingdom develops in the following order: At the bottom
there is an enormous power of propagation with a
complete absence of anything resembling sexual love
(owing to the absence even of division into sexes).
Farther on, among the more perfect organisms, sexual
differentiation, together with its corresponding sexual
attraction, makes its appearance. At first the attraction is
extremely weak, but later it gradually increases in further
stages of organic development, as the power of propaga-

tion diminishes (i.e., attraction is in direct ratio to the perfection of the organization and in inverse ratio to the power of propagation), until finally, at the very peak—in humans—the most powerful possible sexual love makes its appearance, even to the complete exclusion of propagation. So, if in this way, at the two extremes of animal existence we find on the one hand propagation without any sexual love, and on the other hand sexual love without any propagation, then it is perfectly clear that these two phenomena cannot be bonded indissolubly with one another. It is clear that each of them possesses its own independent significance, and that the meaning of the one cannot consist in its being a means to the other. The result is the same if we examine sexual love exclusively in the human world, where it is incomparably greater than in the animal world, and where it assumes that individual character by power of which *just this* person of the other sex possesses for the lover absolute significance, as unique and irreplaceable, as a very end in itself.

II

At this point we encounter the popular theory which, while generally acknowledging sexual love as the means of the generic instinct, or as an instrument of propagation, endeavors in particular to explain the individualization of the feeling of love in humans as a sort of artifice or delusion, employed by nature or the will of the universe for the attainment of its own special ends. In the human world, where individual peculiarities receive far greater significance than in the animal and vegetable kingdoms, nature (otherwise the will of the universe, the will to existence, or the unconscious or supraconscious spirit of the universe) has in view not merely the preservation of the species, but also the realization within its limits of a multitude of possible particular or specific types and individual characters. But besides this general end—the exhibiting of as complete a diversity of forms as possible—human life, understood as historical progress, has the task of elevating and perfecting human nature. This demands not only that there should be the greatest possible diversity of specimens of humanity, but that there should appear in the world the *best* examples of it, which are valuable not only in themselves, as individual types, but also for their elevating and ameliorating influence upon the rest. So, then, besides the propagation of the human species, that power—no matter what we term it—which sets in motion the process of the universe and of history is interested not only that there should continually be born into the world human individuals in accordance with their species, but also that there should be born *these* specific and, as far as possible, significant individualities. But, for this, simple propagation by way of a casual and indifferent union of persons of the opposite sex is insufficient; for an individually *specific* production the combination of individually *specific* producers is necessary, and consequently general sexual attraction, which serves reproduction of the species among animals, is insufficient. Seeing that in humanity the matter concerns not only the production of posterity in general, but also the production of *that* posterity most suitable for the ends of the world, and seeing that a given person can produce this requisite posterity, not with every person of the opposite sex, but only with a specific one, then this one must also possess for him a special attractive power, must appear to him something exceptional, irreplaceable, unique and capable of affording the highest bliss. Here then is that individualization and exaltation of the sexual instinct, by which human love is distinguished from animal. Yet it, like the latter, is awakened in us by an alien power, though it may also be a higher power, for its own ends foreign to our consciousness. It is awakened as an irrational fateful passion, taking possession of us and vanishing like a mirage at the passing of the need for it.[2]

If this theory were correct, if the individualization and elevation of the feeling of love were to possess the whole of its meaning, its sole reason and end outside of this feeling, then it would logically follow that the degree of this individualization and elevation of affection, or the power of love, would be found to be in direct ratio with the degree in which the posterity resulting from it is typical and significant. The more eminent the posterity the more powerful would have to be the love of the progenitors, and conversely, the more powerful the love

binding together the two given persons the more remarkable the posterity we should have to anticipate
from them in accordance with this theory. If, speaking
generally, the feeling of love is awakened by the will of
the universe for the sake of a requisite posterity and is
only the *means* for the production of it, then it is understandable that in each given case the power of the
means employed by the mover of the cosmos should be
in proportion to the importance for him of the end to be
attained. The more the will of the universe is interested
in the appearance of its production on earth, the more
powerfully must it attract to each other and bind together the two necessary producers. Let us suppose that
the matter concerns the birth of an earthly genius possessing enormous significance in the historical process.
The higher power directing this process is obviously as
many times more interested in this birth compared with
others as this earthly genius is a rarer phenomenon in
comparison with ordinary mortals. Consequently the
sexual attraction by which the will of the universe (according to this theory) assures for itself in this case the
attainment so important for its end must be so much
more powerful than the ordinary one. Of course, de-
fenders of this theory may repudiate the idea of any
exact quantitative relation between the importance of
the given person and the power of passion in his or her
progenitors, seeing that these qualities do not admit of
exact measurement. But it is quite indisputable (from
the point of view of this theory) that if the will of the

universe is *extraordinarily interested* in the birth of some particular human being, it must take *extraordinary measures* to assure the desired result, i.e., in accordance with the terms of the theory, it must awaken in the progenitors an *extraordinarily powerful* passion, capable of overcoming all obstacles to their union.

In reality, however, we do not find anything of the kind, nor any such correlation between the power of the passion of love and the significance of the posterity. Above all, we encounter a fact, completely inexplicable by this theory, that a most powerful love is very frequently unshared and produces not a great posterity, but no posterity whatsoever. If, as the result of such love, people go into monasteries or end by committing suicide, then why did the will of the universe interested in posterity take so much trouble? But even if the ardent Werther[3] did not kill himself, his unfortunate passion nonetheless remains an inexplicable riddle for the theory of a qualified posterity. The extraordinarily individualized and elevated love of Werther for Charlotte showed (from the point of view of this theory) that it was precisely with Charlotte that he was destined to produce posterity specially important and necessary for humanity, for the sake of which the will of the universe awakened in him this unusual passion. But why was it that this omniscient and omnipotent will did not think out, or was unable to effect, its desired sense also on Charlotte, without whose participation Werther's passion was entirely purposeless and unnecessary? For a substance which functions teleologically *love's labour lost* is a complete absurdity.

Singularly powerful love is for the most part unfortunate, and unfortunate love quite often leads to suicide in one form or another. And each of these numerous suicides due to unfortunate love is a clear refutation of the theory that powerful love is awakened only in order, come what may, to produce the requisite posterity. The importance of such posterity is indicated theoretically by the power of this love, when as a matter of fact in all these cases the power of the love excludes just the very possibility, not only of important posterity, but also of any posterity whatsoever.

The cases of unshared love are too common for us to see in them merely exceptions which might go unnoticed. But if it were so it would help matters little, for in those cases in which a singularly powerful love is shown on both sides, it does not lead up to what is demanded by the theory. In theory Romeo and Juliet ought, in conformity with their great mutual passion, to have given birth to some very great person, at any rate to a Shakespeare, but as a matter of fact, as is well known, it was just the contrary. They did not produce a Shakespeare, as would follow from the theory, but he created them, and moreover without any passion—by way of sexless creativeness. Romeo and Juliet, like the majority of passionate lovers, perished without having produced anyone, but Shakespeare, though he produced them, was born like other great men, not from a pair madly in

27

love but from an ordinary everyday marriage; and though he himself experienced a powerful passion of love, as is plain from his sonnets amongst other things, yet no remarkable posterity resulted from it. The birth of Christopher Columbus was, it may be, still more important for the will of the universe than the birth of Shakespeare; but we know nothing of any special love on the part of his progenitors, whereas we do know about his own powerful passion for the lady Beatriz Enriquez, and, though he had by her an illegitimate son, Diego,[4] this son never did anything great, only writing a biography of his father, which anyone else could have done.

If the whole meaning of love is found in posterity and a higher power governs the affairs of love, then why, instead of taking trouble to unite the lovers, does this power, on the contrary as it were, intentionally hinder this union, as if its task lay just in this, whatever happened, to take away the very possibility of posterity from true lovers. It compels them through a fatal misapprehension to be buried in vaults, drowns them in the Hellespont,[5] and in many other ways brings them to an untimely and childless end. And in those rare cases when a powerful love does not receive a tragic reverse, when the enamored pair live happily on to old age, they nevertheless remain unfruitful. True poetic feeling for reality compelled both Ovid and Gogol to deprive of posterity Philemon and Baucis and likewise Aphanasy Ivanovich and Pulcheria Ivanovna.[6]

It is impossible to recognize a direct correspondence between the power of individual love and the significance of its posterity, when the very existence of posterity as the result of such love is only a rare occurrence. As we have seen: 1) a powerful love quite often remains unshared; 2) when the powerful passion is mutual it leads to a tragic end, without attaining the production of posterity; 3) a happy love, if it is very powerful, likewise usually remains unfruitful. And in those rare cases when an unusually powerful love does produce posterity, this latter proves to be very ordinary. As a general rule, having almost no exceptions, it may be determined that a peculiar intensity of sexual love either does not admit of posterity at all, or only admits of that whose significance does not correspond in the least to the intensity of the feeling of love and to the exceptional character of the relations which gave them birth.

To regard the meaning of sexual love as an expedient for the procreation of children means to recognize this meaning only where such love itself does not exist at all, and, where it does exist, to take from it any meaning and any justification. This so-called theory of love, when compared with the reality, proves to be not an explanation, but a rejection of any kind of explanation.

III

The power governing human life—which some term the will of the universe, others, the unconscious spirit, and which is as a matter of fact Divine Providence—undoubtedly arranges for the timely generating of those providential individuals necessary for its ends. In the long series of generations it arranges obligatory combinations of producers in view of future creations, not merely immediate but also remote ones. For such a providential selection of producers the most varied means are employed, but love in the real meaning of the word, i.e., exceptional, individualized and elevated sexual attraction, does not belong to the number of these means. Biblical history with its true profound realism—which does not exclude, but embodies the ideal meaning of the facts in their empirical details—adds its testimony in this case, as it always does, truthfully and instructively for every person of historical and artistic sense, independently of religious beliefs.

The central fact of biblical history, the birth of the Messiah, more than any other, presupposes the design of Providence in the selecting and uniting of successive producers, and the real, paramount interest of the biblical narratives is concentrated on the various and wondrous fates, by which are arranged the births and combinations of the "fathers of God."[7] But in all this complicated system of means, having determined in the order of historical phenomena the birth of the Messiah, there was no room for love in the proper meaning of the word. Love is, of course, encountered in the Bible, but only as an independent fact and not as an instrument in the process of the genealogy of Christ. The sacred book does not say that Abram took Sarai to wife by force of an ardent love,[8] and in any case Providence must have waited until this love had grown completely cool for the centenarian progenitors to produce a child of faith, not of love. Isaac married Rebekah not for love but in accordance with an earlier formed resolution and the design of his father. Jacob loved Rachel, but this love turned out to be unnecessary for the origin of the Messiah. He was indeed to be born of a son of Jacob—Judah—but the latter was the offspring, not of Rachel but of the unloved wife, Leah. For the production in the given generation of the ancestor of the Messiah, what was necessary was the union of Jacob precisely with Leah; but to attain this union Providence did not awaken in Jacob any powerful passion of love for the future mother of the "father of God"—Judah. Not infringing the liberty of Jacob's heartfelt feeling, the higher power permitted him to love Rachel, but for his necessary union with Leah it made use of means of quite a different kind: the mercenary cunning of a third person—devoted to his own domestic and economic interests—Laban. Judah himself, for the production of the remote ancestors of the Messiah, besides his legitimate posterity, had in his old age to marry his daughter-in-law Tamar. Seeing that such a union was not at all in the natural order of things, and indeed could not take place under ordinary conditions, that end was attained by means of an extremely strange occurrence very seductive to superficial readers of the Bible.[9] Nor in such an occurrence could there be any talk of love. It was not love which combined the priestly harlot Rahab with the Hebrew stranger; she yielded herself to him at first in the course of her profession, and afterwards the casual bond was strengthened by her faith in the power of the new God and in the desire for his patronage for herself and her family. It was not love which united David's great-grandfather, the aged Boaz, with the youthful Moabitess Ruth, and Solomon was begotten not from genuine, profound love, but only from the casual, sinful caprice of a sovereign who was growing old.

In sacred, as well as in general history, sexual love is not a means to, or the instrument of, historical ends; it does not subserve the human species. That is why, when subjective feeling tells us that love is an independent good and that it possesses an absolute value of its own for our personal existence, then this feeling corresponds also in objective reality with the fact that a powerful, individualized love never exists as an instrument of service for the ends of the species, which are attained apart from it. In general history, as in sacred history, sexual love (in the real sense of the word) plays no role in, and shows no direct influence upon, the historical process: its positive significance must have its roots in individual life.

What then is the meaning it possesses here?

The Meaning of Love

1. [Genesis 7:21]

2. I have stated a general view of the theory I am rejecting, not delaying over the secondary aspects, which it presents in Schopenhauer, Hartmann and others. In his pamphlet, "The Basic Mover of Heredity," (Moscow: 1891) Walter attempts to prove, by the facts of history, that great human beings are born as the fruit of a powerful mutual love.

3. Here and farther on I illustrate my argument chiefly from great works of literature. They are preferable to examples from real life, seeing that they exhibit not isolated phenomena but whole types. [Werther is the hero of Goethe's *The Sorrows of Young Werther* (1774).]

4. [Diego was actually the legitimate son of Columbus. The illegitimate son and author of the biography of his father was Ferdinand (1488–1539).]

5. [Leander used to swim across the Hellespont to meet his lover, Hero. After Leander perishes in a storm, Hero drowns herself.]

6. [Philemon and Baucis are portrayed in Ovid's *Metamorphoses*. Aphanasy Ivanovich and Pulcheria Ivanovna are heroes in Nikolai Gogol's story "Old World Landowners" (1835).]

7. Thus are termed in ecclesiastical language pre-eminently Joachim and Anna, but the other ancestors of the Mother of God also bear this appellation among some ecclesiastical writers.

8. Apparently this is excluded by the well known occurrence in Egypt, which would have been psychologically impossible in the case of a powerful love. [Genesis 12. Fearing for his safety Abram asks Sarai to pretend she is his sister when they enter Egypt. Genesis 21:1–7. At the time of Isaac's birth to Abraham and Sarah, he is 100 and she ninety.]

9. [Genesis 38. Tamar disguises herself as a concubine and sleeps with her father-in-law, after which she conceives twins.]

CHAPTER 2

I

Both in animals and in humans, sexual love is the highest flowering of individual life. But since in animals the life of the species decidedly outweighs that of the individual, then even the highest effort of the individual tends only to benefit the generic process. This is not so that sexual attraction might be only a means for the simple reproduction or propagation of organisms, but that by the aid of sexual rivalry and selection it might serve also for the production of *more perfect* organisms. People have endeavored to attribute the same significance to sexual love in the human world, but, as we have seen, quite fruitlessly. For in humanity individuality possesses an independent significance, and cannot, in its most powerful expression, be merely an instrument of ends of the historical process external to it. Or, to say it better, the true end of the historical process is not of such a nature that human personality could serve merely as a passive and transient instrument of it.

35

Conviction of the absolute worth of the human being is not based on self-conceit or on the empirical fact that we do not know any other more perfect being in the order of nature. The absolute worth of the human being consists in the indubitable presence in him of the absolute form (image) of *rational* consciousness. Conscious, like an animal, of those states experienced and being experienced, discerning among them this or that connection, and, on the basis of this connection, anticipating in his mind future states, a human, *above and beyond this*, possesses the capacity to evaluate his states and acts, and all kinds of facts in general, in their relation not only to other isolated facts, but also to universal ideal norms. His consciousness, over and above the phenomena of life, is also determined by a *rational understanding of truth*. Conforming his actions to this higher consciousness, the human may infinitely perfect his life and nature, *without departing from the limits of human form*. Therefore he is both the highest being of the natural world and the real end of the process of the creation of the world. For besides this being, which is itself eternal and absolute truth, the one among all the others which is capable of discerning and realizing the truth in itself, there is a higher one—not in a relative, but in the absolute sense. What rational basis can be conceived for the creation of new things, in essence more perfect forms, when there is already a form capable of infinite self-perfection, able to make room for all the fulness of absolute content? With the appearance of such a form further progress can consist only in new degrees of its own development, and not in its replacement by any creations whatsoever of another kind, by other unprecedented forms of existence. In this is the essential distinction between cosmogonic and historical processes. The first (until the appearance of humans) creates ever newer and newer species of beings, in whose presence previous ones in part die out as unsuccessful experiments and in part still coexist together with the new in an external way, casually colliding without forming any *real* unity because of their lack of a general consciousness which would bind them with each other and with the cosmic past. Such general consciousness makes its appearance in humanity. In the world of animals the succession of higher forms from lower ones, with all their rightness and suitability, is a fact absolutely external and alien to the animals themselves, a fact quite nonexistent for them. The elephant and the ape can know nothing about the complicated process of geological and biological transformations which have conditioned their actual appearance on earth. A comparatively higher degree of development of a particular and isolated consciousness does not here signify any progress in *general* consciousness, which is as absolutely absent in these intelligent animals as in a stupid oyster. The complicated brain of a higher mammal serves as little for the self-enlightenment of nature in its entirety as do the rudimentary nerve-ganglia of any worm. In humanity, on the contrary, through an elevated individual consciousness, religious and scientific, universal consciousness progresses. The individual mind is here not merely the organ of personal life, but likewise the organ of remembrance and divination for the whole of humanity, and even for the whole of nature. The Hebrew who wrote: *These are the generations of the heaven and of the earth*, and further: *This is the book of the generations of Adam*,[1] was expressing not only his personal and national consciousness. Through him first shone forth in the world the truth of the unity of the whole universe and of all humanity.[2] And all further advances of consciousness consist solely in the development and embodiment of this truth, for they have no reason and cannot possibly go beyond this *all-embracing* form. What else can the most perfect astronomy and geology do but restore completely the genesis of the heaven and the earth; in just the same way the highest task of historical knowledge can only be to restore "the book of the generations of Adam," i.e., the successive genetic bond in the life of humanity. And finally, our creative activity can possess no higher end than to embody in perceptible images this unity of heaven, earth and humanity created and proclaimed from the beginning. *All truth*—the positive unity of all—is pledged from the beginning in the living consciousness of humans, and gradually realized in the life of humanity, with conscious succession (for truth *unmindful of its kindred* is not truth). Thanks to the boundless expansivity and indissolubility of the successive consciousness, a human being, still remaining his same self, may attain and realize all the limitless fulness of being, and therefore no higher species of beings in place of him are either necessary or possible. Within the limits of his given reality a human is only a part of nature; but constantly and consistently he is infringing these limits. In his spiritual offspring—religion and science, morality and art—the human being is revealed as the center of the universal consciousness of nature, the soul of the world, the potentiality of the absolute unity-of-the-all coming to realization, and, consequently, above him there can be only this same absolute in its perfect act or eternal being, that is God.

II

The superiority of the human being to the other creatures of nature—his capacity to recognize and realize the truth—is not only generic but also individual: *each* human is capable of recognizing and realizing truth, each may become a living reflection of the absolute whole, a conscious and independent organ of the universal life. In the rest of nature there is also truth (or the Divine image), but only in its objective communality, unknown to the particular creatures. It forms them and acts in them and through them—as a fateful power, as the very law of their being, unknown to them, to which they are subject involuntarily and unconsciously. For

themselves, in their own internal feeling and consciousness, they are unable to rise above their given particular
existence; they find themselves only in their particularity, in separation from the *all*—consequently, *outside the
truth*. And therefore the truth or the universal can triumph here only in the replacement of generations, in
the permanence of the species and in the destruction of
the individual life, which does not accommodate the
truth in itself. Human individuality, therefore, for the
very reason that it can accommodate the truth in itself,
is not abrogated by it, but is preserved and enhanced in
the triumph of truth.

　　Even so, in order for the individual being to find in
the truth—in the unity-of-the-all—his or her own justification and affirmation, mere consciousness of the
truth on the individual's part is insufficient; he must also
be in the truth. But originally and immediately the individual human being, like the animal, is not in the truth.
He finds himself as an individualized infinitesimal par-
ticle of the universal whole, and this his particular being
he affirms in his egoism as a whole for itself, wishing to
be all in separation from the all—outside the truth.
Egoism, as the real, basic source of individual life, per-
meates and directs the whole of this life and determines
everything concrete in it, and therefore theoretical consciousness of the truth alone can by no means outweigh
and abrogate it. So long as the living power of egoism in
humans does not encounter another living power opposed to it, consciousness of the truth is only an exter-

nal illumination, a reflection of an alien light. If a human could only in this sense accommodate the truth, then the bond between it and his individuality would not be internal and indissoluble. His authentic being, remaining, like that of the animal, outside the truth, would be, like the animal, doomed (in its subjectivity) to destruction, being preserved only as an idea in the thought of the absolute mind.

Truth as a living power that takes possession of the internal being of a human and actually rescues him from false self-assertion is termed Love. Love as the actual abrogation of egoism is the real justification and salvation of individuality. Love is greater than rational consciousness, yet without the latter it could not act as an internal saving power, elevating and not abrogating individuality. Only thanks to a rational consciousness (or, what is the same thing, a consciousness of the truth) can a human being discriminate his very self, i.e., his true individuality, from his egoism, and therefore sacrifice this egoism, and surrender himself to love. In doing so he finds not merely a living, but also a life-giving power, and does not forfeit his individual being together with his egoism, but on the contrary makes it eternal. In the world of animals, as a result of their lack of proper rational consciousness, the truth, which realizes itself in love, does not find in them any internal point of support for its activity and can act only directly, as an external fateful power. It takes possession of them like blind instruments, for ends of the universe alien to them. Here love appears as a one-sided triumph of the general, the generic, over the individual, inasmuch as in animals their individuality coincides with their egoism in the immediacy of their particular being, and therefore perishes together with it.

III

The meaning of human love, speaking generally, is *the justification and salvation of individuality through the sacrifice of egoism*. On this general basis we can also complete our particular task: to explain the meaning of sexual love. For good reason sexual relations are not merely termed love, but are also generally acknowledged to represent love *par excellence*, being the type and ideal of all other kinds of love (cf. the *Song of Songs* and the *Apocalypse*).

The falsehood and evil of egoism by no means consist in the fact that the egoist values himself too highly, credits himself with absolute significance and infinite worth. In this he is correct, because every human subject, as an independent center of living powers, as a potentiality (possibility) of infinite perfection, as a being capable in consciousness and in his life of accommodating absolute truth—every person, as such, possesses absolute significance and worth. In every human being there is something absolutely irreplaceable, and one cannot value oneself too highly. (In the words of the gospel: "What shall a man give in exchange for his soul?")[3] Failure to recognize one's own absolute significance is equivalent to a denial of human worth; this is a basic error and the origin of all unbelief. If one is so faint-hearted that he is powerless even to believe in himself, how can he believe in anything else? The basic falsehood and evil of egoism lie not in this absolute self-consciousness and self-evaluation of the subject, but in the fact that, ascribing to himself in all justice an absolute significance, he unjustly refuses to others this same significance. Recognizing himself as a center of life (which as a matter of fact he is), he relegates others to the circumference of his own being and leaves them only an external and relative value.

It is self-evident that in abstract theoretical consciousness every person who has not lost his senses always admits for others full enjoyment of equal rights with himself. But in his living consciousness, in his innermost feelings and in deeds, he asserts an infinite difference and complete incommensurability between himself and others: he himself is everything, they themselves are nothing. Meanwhile, especially under such an exclusionary self-assertion, the human being cannot be in reality what he affirms himself to be. That absolute significance, that absolute value, which in general he justly acknowledges for himself, but unjustly denies for others, possesses in itself only a potential character—it is only a possibility, demanding its own realization. God *is* all, i.e., he possesses in one absolute act all positive content, the whole fulness of being. A human being (in general and every individual being in particular), being in fact only *this* and not *another*, may *become* all, only by doing away, in his consciousness and life, with that internal boundary which separates him from another. "This" may become the "all" only *together with others*; only together with others can an individual realize his absolute significance—become an inseparable and irreplaceable part of the universal whole, an independent, living and original organ of the absolute life. True individuality is a certain specific likeness of the unity-of-the-all, a certain specific means of receiving and appropriating to oneself all that is other. Asserting himself apart from all that is other, a human by that very act divests his own real existence of meaning, deprives himself of the true content of life and reduces his individuality to an empty form. In this way egoism is by no means the self-consciousness and self-affirmation of individuality, but on the contrary its self-negation and destruction.

Metaphysical, physical, historical and social conditions in human existence modify and mitigate our egoism in all ways, placing powerful and varied obstacles in the way of its manifestation in a pure form and in all its terrible consequences. But all this complicated system of hindrances and correctives, foreordained by Providence and realized by natural history, leaves untouched the very basis of egoism, which perpetually peeps out from under cover of personal and public morality, and on occasion manifests itself with perfect distinctness. There is only one power which can from within undermine egoism at the root, and really does undermine it, namely love, and chiefly sexual love. The falsehood and evil of egoism consist in the exclusive acknowledgment of absolute significance for oneself and in the denial of it for others. Reason shows us that this is unfounded and unjust, but simply by the facts love directly abrogates such an unjust relation, compelling us not by abstract consciousness, but by an internal emotion and the will of life to recognize for ourselves the absolute significance of another. Recognizing in love the truth of another, not abstractly, but essentially, transferring in deed the center of our life beyond the limits of our empirical personality, we by so doing reveal and realize our own real truth, our own absolute significance, which consists just in our capacity to transcend the borders of our factual phenomenal being, in our capacity to live not only in ourselves, but also in another.

Every kind of love is the manifestation of this capacity, but not every kind realizes it to the same degree, nor does every kind as radically undermine egoism. Egoism is a power not only real but basic, rooted in the deepest center of our being, and from thence permeating and embracing the whole of our reality—a power, acting uninterruptedly in all aspects and particulars of our existence. In order genuinely to undermine egoism, it is necessary to oppose to it a love equally concretely specific, permeating the whole of our being and taking possession of everything in it. So then this other force, which is to emancipate our individuality from the fetters of egoism, must possess a correlation with the whole of that individuality, must be equally real and concrete, a completely objectified subject like ourselves. Moreover, in order to really be another it must in everything be distinguished from us; i.e., possessing all that essential content which we also possess, it must possess it in another means or mode, in another form. In this way every manifestation of our being, every vital act would encounter in this other a corresponding, but not identical, manifestation, in such a way that the relation of the one to the other would be a complete and continual exchange, a complete and continual affirmation of oneself in the other, with perfect reciprocity and communion. Only then will egoism be undermined and abrogated; abolished, not in principle alone, but in all its concrete reality. Only under the action of this, so to speak, chemical union of two beings, of the same nature and of equal significance, but *on all sides* distinct as to form, is the creation possible (both in the natural order and in the spiritual order) of a new human being, the real realization of true human individuality. Such a union, or at least the closest approximation to it, we find in sexual love, for which reason we attach to it exceptional significance, as the necessary basis of all further perfection, as the inescapable and permanent condition under which alone a human can really be in the truth.

IV

Recognizing fully the great significance and the high worth of the other kinds of love by which a false spirituality and an impotent moralism would desire to replace sexual love, we see, nevertheless, that only this latter satisfies the two basic demands without which the resolute abrogation of selfishness in a complete living interchange with others is an impossibility. In all other kinds of love there is lacking either homogeneity, equality and reciprocity between the lover and the loved one, or the all-round diversity of those qualities which complete each other.

Thus, in mystical love the object of love comes in the long run to an absolute indistinction, which swallows up the human individuality. Here egoism is abrogated only in that very insufficient sense in which it is abrogated when a person falls into a state of very deep sleep (to which it is compared in the Upanishads and the Vedas, where at times also the union of individual souls is directly identified with the universal spirit). Between a living human and the mystical "Abyss" of absolute indistinction, owing to the complete heterogeneity and incommensurability of these magnitudes, not only living interchange, but even simple compatibility cannot exist. If there is an object of love, then there is no lover—he has disappeared, lost himself, is sunk as it were in profound and dreamless slumber; when he comes back to himself, the object of love vanishes, and instead of absolute indistinction a many-colored multiform of real life reigns on a background of his own egoism, embellished with spiritual vainglory. For the rest, history knows of such mystics and of whole mystical schools in which the object of love has not been conceived as absolute indistinction, but has assumed concrete forms which admitted of living relations to them; but—very remarkably—these relations received here a perfectly distinct and consistently sustained character of sexual love. . . .

Parental love—and in particular maternal love— both in its power of feeling and in the concreteness of its object, approximates sexual love, but for other reasons cannot possess equal significance with it for human individuality. It is dependent on the fact of propagation and the law of the succession of generations, which rule over animal existence but do not possess, or in any case do not need to possess, the same significance for human life. Among animals the succeeding generation directly and quickly abrogates its predecessors and convicts them of the absurdity of their existence, to be straightaway, in its own turn, convicted of the same absurdity at the hands of its own offspring. Maternal love in humanity, though sometimes attaining a high degree of self-sacrifice, such as we do not find in the love of a mother-hen, is a remnant, undoubtedly still necessary, of this order of things. In any case, it is beyond doubt that in maternal love there cannot be full reciprocity and living interchange, for the very reason that the lover and the loved ones belong to different generations, that for the latter life is in the future with new independent interests and tasks, in the midst of which representatives of the past appear only like pale shadows. It is sufficient that parents cannot be for their children the end of their life, in the same sense that children are for their parents.

The mother whose whole soul is wrapped up in her children does of course sacrifice her egoism, but at the same time she loses her individuality; and if in the children maternal love maintains its individuality, it preserves and even strengthens egoism. Besides this, in maternal love there is not, properly speaking, the recognition of the absolute significance of the beloved, the recognition of its true individuality, because for the mother, though her child is dearer than all, yet it is only just as *her* child, not otherwise than in other animals; i.e., here the so-called recognition of the absolute significance of another is in reality made dependent on an external physiological bond.

Still less can the remaining kinds of sympathetic feelings possess any claim to take the place of sexual love. Friendship between persons of one and the same sex is lacking in the overall difference in form, in qualities which complete each other. And if, nevertheless, such a friendship attains a peculiar intensity, then it is

49

transmuted into an unnatural surrogate for sexual love. As for patriotism and love of humanity, these feelings, despite all their importance, cannot in themselves as such do away, in a vital and concrete fashion, with egoism, owing to the incommensurability of the lover and the beloved: humanity, and even the nation, cannot be for the individual being the selfsame concrete object as he is himself. To sacrifice his own existence for his nation or for humanity is, of course, possible, but to create out of himself a new human being, to develop and realize a true human individuality on the basis of this extensive love, is impossible. In it, at the real center, there remains all the same his old egotistical "I," while nation and humanity are relegated to the periphery of consciousness as ideal objects. The same must be said of love for science, art and the rest.

Having indicated in a few words the true meaning of sexual love and its superiority to other kindred feelings, I must explain why it is so feebly realized in reality, and show in what way the full realization of it is possible.

1. [Genesis 2:4 and 5:1.]

2. If it is said that these words are divinely inspired, that will be no refutation but only a translation of my meaning into theological language.

3. [Matthew 16:26 and Mark 8:37.]

CHAPTER 3

I

The meaning and worth of love, as a feeling, is that it really forces us, with all our being, to acknowledge for *another* the same absolute central significance which, because of the power of our egoism, we are conscious of only in our own selves. Love is important not as one of our feelings, but as the transfer of all our interest in life from ourselves to another, as the shifting of the very center of our personal lives. This is characteristic of every kind of love, but predominantly of sexual love;[1] it is distinguished from other kinds of love by greater intensity, by a more engrossing character, and by the possibility of more complete overall reciprocity. Only this love can lead to the real and indissoluble union of two lives into one; only of it do the words of Holy Writ say: "They shall be one flesh," i.e., shall become one real being.[2]

Feeling demands such a fulness of union, internal and definitive, but the matter does not ordinarily go

51

further than this subjective demand and aspiration, and even this is transient. As a matter of fact, instead of the poetry of eternal and central union, there occurs only a more or less lasting, but for all that temporal, more or less close, but for all that external, superficial rapprochement of two finite beings within the narrow framework of the prose of everyday existence. The object of love does not in reality preserve that absolute significance which is attached to it by the dream of love. From the outsider's point of view this is clear from the very beginning; but the unintentional tinge of mockery, which inevitably accompanies the outsider's relation to lovers, turns out to be only the anticipation of their own disenchantment. At one stroke, or little by little, the intense emotion of the enthusiasm of love passes away, and yet all is well, if, having manifested itself in such love, the energy of altruistic feeling is not wasted and purposeless, but, only having lost its concentration and spirit of high emprise, is transferred in a divided and weakened form to the children, who are begotten and reared for a repetition of this same illusion. I say illusion—from the point of view of *individual* life and of the absolute significance of human personality—though I fully acknowledge the necessity and usefulness of the procreation of children and the succession of generations for the progress of humanity in its collective existence. But of love in the strict sense of the word there is here no question. The coincidence of a powerful passion of love with the successful procreation of children is merely fortuitous, and even so is sufficiently rare; historical and everyday experience illustrate beyond doubt that children may be successfully begotten, ardently loved and excellently reared by their parents, though these latter had never been in love with each other. Consequently, the collective and universal interests of humanity, bound to the succession of generations, do not at all demand any lofty intense emotion of love. And meanwhile in the life of the individual this supreme flowering of love proves to be a barren blossom. Love's primordial power here loses all its meaning, when its object is degraded from the height of the absolute center of immortal individuality to the level of a fortuitous and easily replaced means for the production of a new generation of human beings, a generation that may be a little better or may be a little worse, but is in any case relative and transitory.

If therefore we look only at what ordinarily exists, at the actual outcome of love, then we are forced to acknowledge that love is a dream, which temporarily possesses our being and then disappears without ever carrying over into actuality (since the procreation of children is not strictly an act of love). But recognizing from the conspicuous power of love that its ideal meaning is not realized in reality, must we therefore acknowledge that it is *unrealizable*?

By the very nature of the human being, who in his rational consciousness, moral freedom and capacity for self-perfection possesses infinite possibilities, we have no right to reckon beforehand that any task whatsoever would be unrealizable, unless it contains in itself a logical contradiction or want of conformity with the general meaning of the universe and the harmonious course of cosmic and historical development.

It would be completely unjust to deny the possibility of realizing love merely on the basis that hitherto it never has been realized: you must know that many other things were once in the same situation, for instance, all sciences and arts, the civic community, our control of the powers of nature. Even rational consciousness itself, before becoming a fact in humans, was only a perplexed and unsuccessful aspiration in the world of animals. How many geological and biological epochs passed away in unsuccessful attempts to create a brain qualified to become the organ for the embodiment of rational thought? Love is as yet for humans what reason was for the animal world: it exists in its beginnings, or as an earnest of what it will be, but not as yet in actual fact. And if enormous world periods—testifying to the yet unrealized reason—did not hinder it from being realized in the end, still less does the nonrealization of love, in the course of the comparatively few thousands of years experienced by historical humanity, in any way give us the right to infer anything whatever against its future realization. It follows only that it is well to remember that, if the reality of rational consciousness has manifested itself in humans but not through humans, the realization of love, as the highest stage towards the true life of that same humanity, must issue not only in humanity but *through it*.

The task of love consists in *justifying in deed* that meaning of love which at first is given only in feeling. It demands such a union of two given finite natures as would create out of them one absolute ideal personality. This task not only does not contain in itself any kind of contradiction or nonconformity with the meaning of the universe, but it is directly posed by our spiritual nature. The peculiar character of this nature consists just in a human being's ability, while remaining the selfsame human being, to accommodate absolute content in his own proper form, to become an absolute personality. But in order to be filled with absolute content (which in the language of religion is termed eternal life or the kingdom of God), that same human form must be restored in its entirety (integrated). In the empirical reality of the human being, as such, this is by no means so—he exists only in a specific onesidedness and finiteness, as a male or female individuality (and already on this basis all other distinctions are developed). However, a true human in the fulness of his ideal personality, obviously, cannot be merely male or merely female, but must be the higher unity of both. To realize this unity, to create the true human being as a free unity of the male and female principles, preserving their formal individualization but having surmounted their essential separateness and divergence—this is the proper immediate *task* of love.

Considering those conditions necessary for the actual achievement of this task, we are convinced that only the nonfulfillment of these conditions brings love to perpetual wreck and forces us to acknowledge it as an illusion.

II

The first step to the successful completion of any task is a conscious and faithful statement of it; but the task of love has never been stated consciously, and therefore never resolved, as it should have been. People have looked, and do look, upon love only as a given fact, as a state (normal in some, unhealthy in others) which is experienced by a human, but which imposes no duty upon him. The truth is that there are two tasks involved here: physical possession of the person beloved and living union with him. The latter task imposes certain obligations. At once the matter is subject to the laws of animal nature on the one hand, and to the laws of civic and community life on the other, while from the very beginning to the very end love, if left to itself, vanishes like a mirage. Of course, love is before all a fact of nature (or a gift of God), a natural process arising independently of us; but it does not follow from this that we could not and should not relate consciously to it and independently direct this natural process to higher ends. The gift of speech is likewise a natural attribute of humans; language, like love, has not been thought up. Nevertheless, it would be exceedingly sad to relate to it merely as a natural process which goes on in us of its own accord, as if we speak as birds sing and should give ourselves up to natural combinations of sounds and words for the expression of feelings and scenes which involuntarily pass through our souls, but should never make of language an instrument for the coherent imparting of certain thoughts, a means for the attainment of rational ends we consciously set ourselves. Under an exclusively passive and unconscious relation to the gift of speech, humans would not be able to organize either science or art or civic community, and even language itself, as a result of insufficient application of this gift, would fail to develop and would stop short after a few of its rudimentary manifestations. Such significance as the *word* possesses for the formation of human society and culture, *love* also possesses in a still greater degree for the creation of true human individuality. And if in the social and cultural domain we observe progress, indubitable though slow, then human individuality from the very beginning of historical times up to the present has remained unchanged within its actual narrow limitations. The first cause of this difference is that we relate ever more and more consciously and independently to verbal reality and the products of the word, while love, as formerly, is left entirely in the obscure regions of tumultuous affections and involuntary attractions.

Just as the true significance of the word consists not in the process of speaking in itself, but in *what* is said—in the revealing of things by reason through words or ideas—so the true significance of love consists not in the simple experience of this feeling, but in what is accomplished by means of it—in the act of love. For love it is insufficient to feel for itself the absolute significance of the beloved object, but it is necessary to effectively impart or communicate this significance to the object, to be united with it in the actual creation of an absolute individuality. The highest task of true language is already foreordained by the very nature of words, which inevitably represent general and permanent ideas, not separate and transient impressions; consequently, being already in themselves the bond of many in one, they bring us to the comprehension of universal meaning. In a similar fashion the highest task of love is already marked out beforehand in the very feeling of love itself, which inevitably and prior to any kind of realization introduces its object into the sphere of absolute individuality, sees it in ideal light, and has faith in its absoluteness. Thus in both cases (in the realm of verbal cognition and likewise in the realm of love), the task consists not in thinking up anything whatsoever completely new out of one's own mind, but only in consistently carrying farther and right to the end what has already been given in germ, in the very nature of the act, in the very basis of the process. But whereas the word has developed and is developing in humanity, with regard to love people have come to a standstill and to this day have not passed beyond a few natural rudiments, and even these are poorly understood in their true meaning.

III

It is well known to everyone that in love there inevitably exists a special *idealization* of the beloved object, which presents itself to the lover in a completely different light from that in which outsiders see it. I speak here of light not merely in a metaphorical sense; it is a matter not only of a special moral and intellectual evaluation, but also of a special sensuous perception: the lover really *sees*, visually perceives, what others do not. And if for him too this light of love quickly disappears, yet does it follow from this that it was false, that it was only a subjective illusion?

The true being of the human being in general and of each human in particular is not exhausted by his given empirical manifestations—it is impossible from any point of view to contravene this position on a solid and rational basis. For the materialist and the sensualist, no less than for the spiritualist and the idealist, what appears is not equivalent to what is; and when it is a matter of two different views of what seems to be, then it is always a legitimate question which of these two views is more in harmony with what is, or better expresses the nature of things. For what seems to be, or visibility in general, is really a relation or reciprocity between seer and seen, and, consequently, is determined by their respective characters. The external world of the human and the external world of the mole—both consist only of relative phenomena or appearances; yet hardly anyone seriously doubts that one of these two apparent worlds is superior to the other, corresponds more to what is nearer to the truth.

We know that a human being, besides his animal material nature, possesses moreover an ideal nature which binds him with absolute truth or with God. Besides the material or empirical content of his life, each human comprises in himself the image of God, i.e., a special form of the absolute content. Theoretically and in the abstract this Divine image is known to us in mind and through reason, but in love it is known in the concrete and in life. And if this revelation of the ideal being, ordinarily concealed by its material manifestation, is not limited in love to merely an internal feeling, but at times becomes noticeable also in the sphere of external feelings, then so much greater is the significance we must acknowledge for love, as being from the very beginning the visible restoration of the Divine image in the material world, the beginning of the embodiment of true ideal humanity. The power of love, passing into the world, transforming and spiritualizing the form of external phenomena, reveals to us its objective might, and after that it is up to us. We ourselves must understand this revelation and take advantage of it, so that it may not remain a passing and enigmatic flash of some mystery.

The psycho-physical process of the restoration of the Divine image in material humanity has no means to perfect itself by itself, apart from us. Its origin, like that of everything better in this world, arises from the realm of unconscious processes and relations obscure to us; there lie the germ and root of the tree of life, but we must foster it with our conscious activity. For the beginning passive receptivity of feeling suffices, but subsequently active faith is necessary, with moral effort and hard work, to keep for oneself, to strengthen and develop this gift of luminous and creative love, in order through it to incarnate in oneself and in another the image of God, and to create out of two infinite and perishable natures one absolute and immortal individuality. If, inevitably and without our own volition, the existent idealization of love reveals to us through empirical appearance a distant ideal image of the beloved object, this is not, of course, only that we might delight in it, but that by power of true faith, active imagination and real creativeness we might transform, in accordance with this true exemplar, the reality not corresponding to it, and might embody it in a real phenomenon.

But who has not at some time had thoughts of this kind about love? The Minnesingers[3] and knights of medieval days, with their powerful faith and weak reason, set their minds at rest by simply identifying their amorous ideal with the given person, shutting their eyes to any manifest discrepancies. This faith was as steadfast and as barren as that stone on which the celebrated knight von Grinvaldus "always in the same position" sat "by the castle of Amalia."[4]

Along with such faith, which only compelled men to reverently contemplate and rapturously sing the praises of their so-called incarnate ideal, medieval love was, of course, bound up with a thirst for exploits. But these warlike and destructive feats, since they were in no way related to the ideal which had inspired them, could not contribute to its realization. Even that pallid knight who had wholly yielded to the impression which revealed heavenly beauty to him and did not confound it with earthly manifestation was inspired by this revelation only to such acts as served more to the detriment of other peoples than to the advantage and glory of the "eternal feminine."[5]

> *Lumen coeli! Sancta rosa!*
> Cried he wild and ardent,
> And like thunder did his menace
> Overthrow the Moslems.[6]

For the overthrow of the Moslems there was of course no need to possess "a vision, unfathomable to the mind." But this disharmony between the celestial visions of Christianity and the "wild and ardent" powers in real life weighed on all medieval chivalry, till in the end the illustrious last of the knights, Don Quixote de la

Mancha, having shattered many sheep and demolished not a few windmill sails, without having approximated the Tobosan dairy-maid to his ideal Dulcinea, arrived not at a just but only at a negative acknowledgment of his error. And whereas that typical knight [Pushkin's] remained faithful to his vision to the end and "died as one out of his mind,"[7] then Don Quixote from madness passed over only to a sorrowful and hopeless disenchantment with his ideal.

This disenchantment of Don Quixote's was the bequest of chivalry to the new Europe. It acts in us even up to this very day. The idealization of love, having ceased to be the fountainhead of exploits of the mad, no longer inspires us to such deeds. It proves to be only a decoy, constraining us to desire physical and earthly possession, and vanishes as soon as this—anything but ideal—end is attained. Nor does the light of love serve for anyone as a ray of light upon the path towards a lost Paradise. Humans look upon it as the fantastic illumination of a brief amorous "prologue to Heaven,"[8] which later on nature extinguishes in her own good time, as being completely unnecessary for the earthly scene which follows. As a matter of fact this light extinguishes the weakness and unconsciousness of our love, distorting the true order of the matter.

IV

The external union, earthly and in particular physical, does not possess any specific relation to love. It exists without love, and love exists without it. It is necessary for love, not as its indispensable condition and independent end, but only as its final realization. If this realization is set as the end in itself, ahead of the ideal concern of love, it ruins the love. Every kind of external act or fact in itself is nothing; love is something only thanks to its meaning or idea as the restoration of the unity or integrity of the human personality, as the creation of an absolute individuality. The significance of the external acts or facts connected with love, which in themselves are nothing, is determined by their relation to what constitutes love itself and its matter. When a nought is placed after an integer, it increases it tenfold, but when it is placed in front of it, it diminishes or reduces it as much, taking away from its character as an integer and converting it into a decimal fraction; and the more noughts are put in front of the integer, the smaller the fraction becomes, the more nearly it itself approaches nought.

The feeling of love in itself is only an impulse, suggesting to us that we can and ought to restore the integrity of the human being. Each time this sacred spark is kindled in a human heart, all of creation waits groaning and travailing for the first revelation of the glory of the sons of God. But without the activity of the conscious human spirit, the Divine spark is extinguished, and deceived nature creates new generations of the sons of men for new hopes.

These hopes will not be fulfilled until the time when we will desire fully to acknowledge and to realize to the end all that true love demands, all that is comprised in the idea of it. With the conscious relation to love and with the real resolution to accomplish the task it sets, two facts above all appear to be a hindrance, condemning us to impotence and justifying those who count love an illusion. In the feeling of love, according to its basic meaning, we assert the absolute significance of another individuality, and by so doing we assert also the absolute significance of our own. But an absolute individuality cannot be *transient*, and it cannot be *empty*. The inevitability of death and the emptiness of our own life are completely incompatible with that elevated assertion of individuality, one's own and another's, which is contained in the feeling of love. This feeling, if it is powerful and completely conscious, cannot be reconciled with the conviction of the imminent decline and death of the person beloved, and of one's own death. In the meantime this indubitable fact, that all humans always have died and do die, is accepted by everybody or nearly everybody as an absolutely inexorable law. (Even in formal logic it is acceptable to avail oneself of this conviction to establish the model syllogism: "All men are mortal, Caius is a man, therefore Caius is mortal.")[9] Many, it is true, believe in the immortality of the soul; but it is just the feeling of love which best of all shows the inadequacy of this abstract belief. A disembodied soul is not a human, but an angel; we, however, love the human, the entire human individuality, and if love is the beginning of the enlightenment and spiritualization of this individuality, then it necessarily demands its preservation as such, demands the eternal youth and immortality of this specific human being, of this living spirit incarnate in a bodily organism. An angel or pure spirit does not stand in need of enlightenment and spiritualization; only the flesh is enlightened and spiritualized, and it is the necessary object of love. It is possible to picture anything one likes to oneself, but it is possible to love only what is living and concrete, and loving it in reality cannot possibly be reconciled with the conviction of its annihilation.

But if the inevitability of death is incompatible with true love, then immortality is quite incompatible with the emptiness of our life. For the majority of humanity life is only a succession of wearisome mechanical labors and coarse sensuous satisfactions which numb consciousness. And that minority which has the opportunity to concern itself actively, not merely about the means, but also about the ends of life, instead of doing so, utilizes its freedom from mechanical toil chiefly for meaningless and immoral pastimes. I have nothing to add to the emptiness and immorality—even if unwilling and unconscious—of all this transitory life, after its magnificent depiction in *Anna Karenina, The Death of Ivan Ilyitch* and *The Kreutzer Sonata*[10] Returning to my subject, I point only to the obvious consideration, that for *such* a life death is not only inevitable, but even extremely desirable. Is it possible without dreadful anguish even to picture to oneself the existence, prolonged without end, of any society lady, or sportsman, or card-player?

The incompatibility of immortality with *such* an existence is plain at the first glance. But with greater attention we shall have to recognize the same incompatibility relative to other existences, apparently fuller of meaning. If instead of a society lady or a card-player we take, at the opposite pole, great men, geniuses who have endowed humanity with immortal productions or have changed the destiny of nations, then we see that the content and historical fruits of their lives possess significance only as given once and for ever, and that these would lose all meaning under an endlessly prolonged individual existence of these geniuses on earth. The immortality of the production, it is plain, in no wise demands, and even in itself excludes, the uninterrupted immortality of the individuality which has produced it. Is it possible to picture to oneself Shakespeare endlessly composing his dramas, or Newton endlessly occupied in studying the mechanics of the heavens, to say nothing of the absurdity of an endless continuance of such activities as those for which Alexander the Great and Napoleon were famous? It is evident that art, science and politics, which give content to the diverse impulses of the human spirit and satisfy the temporary historical demands of humanity, do not by any means communicate the absolute, self-sufficient content of human *individuality*, and therefore stand in no need of its immortality. Of this only love stands in need, and only love can attain it. True love is that which not only affirms in subjective feeling the absolute significance of human individuality in another and in oneself, but also justifies this absolute significance in reality, really rescues us from the inevitability of death and fills out our life with an absolute content.

1. I call sexual love, for want of a better term, the exclusive attachment (one-sided as well as mutual) between persons of different sexes which makes possible the relation between them of husband and wife, but in no wise do I prejudge by this the question of the importance of the physical side of the matter.

2. [Genesis 2:24.]

3. [The Minnesingers were German lyric poets and singers between the twelfth and fourteenth centuries.]

4. [From a satirical poem, "A German Ballad," written in 1854 by Kuzma Prutkov (Aleksei Zhemchuzhnikov) based on a Zhukovski translation of Schiller's "Ritter Toggenburg."]

5. [The "Eternal Feminine" is a central feature of Solovyov's philosophy. For an excellent treatment of the concept see Samuel D. Cioran, *Vladimir Solov'ev and the Knighthood of the Divine Sophia* (1977).]

6. [These lines come from a famous poem by Aleksandr Pushkin, "There lived a poor knight in the world." Written in 1829 the poem did not appear during Pushkin's lifetime. It is sometimes referred to as "The Legend." The poem was reworked and incorporated into an unfinished play "Scenes of Knightly Times" (1835).]

7. [This line is contained only in the 1835 version of Pushkin's poem.]

8. [The opening part of Goethe's, *Faust*.]

9. [Aristotle in his *Analytics* uses the syllogism: All men are mortal, Socrates is a man, therefore: Socrates is mortal. The version used here is found in Tolstoi's novel, *The Death of Ivan Ilyich*, attributed to a Russian translation of Johann Kiesewetter's textbook of logic.]

10. Our "society," including many worldly ladies, has read these works, and in particular *The Kreutzer Sonata*, with delight. But hardly ever has one of them after such a reading declined any invitation to a ball—so difficult is it for an Ethic, even in perfect artistic form, to modify the actual behavior of general society. [All are works by Lev Tolstoi: *Anna Karenina* (1877); *The Death of Ivan Ilyich* (1886); *The Kreutzer Sonata* (1890).]

CHAPTER 4

I

"Dionysus and Hades—one and the same,"[1] said a profound thinker of the ancient world. Dionysus, the youthful and blooming god of material existence in the full exercise of its exuberant powers, the god of nature stimulated and fruitful, is the selfsame as Hades, the pallid ruler of the gloomy and silent kingdom of departed shades. The god of life and the god of death— one and the same god. This is a truth beyond dispute for the world of natural organisms. The fulness of life's powers bubbling over in the individual being is not its own life, but an alien life, the life of a species indifferent to it and merciless, a fulness which for it is death. In the lower divisions of the animal kingdom this is completely plain. Here individuals exist only to produce posterity and then to die; in many species they do not survive the act of propagation and die on the spot, while in others they survive only for a very short time. But if this bond between birth and death, between the preservation of the species and the perishing of the individual, is the law of nature, then, on the other hand, nature itself in its progressive development is ever more and more limiting and relaxing this its own law. The necessity for the individual to serve as a means for the preservation of the race and to die when it has fulfilled this service remains; but the action of this necessity is manifested ever less and less directly and exclusively in proportion to the perfection of the organic forms, in proportion to the increasing independence and consciousness of the individual beings. Thus the law of the identity of Dionysus and Hades—of the life of the species and individual death or, what is the same thing, the law of the contradiction and antagonism between the species and the individual—acts most powerfully at the lower levels of the organic world, relaxing more and more with the development of higher forms. But if this is so, then with the appearance of the highest organic form, investing with self-consciousness and spontaneity an individual being which distinguishes itself from nature and relates to it as to an object, and is in consequence capable of internal freedom from the demands of the species—with the appearance of such a being must not the end of this tyranny of the species over the individual be near at hand? If in the biological process nature is striving ever more and more to limit the law of death, then must not humans in the historical process completely abrogate this law?

It is self-evident that so long as a human being

propagates like an animal, he will die like an animal. But on the other hand, it is equally clear that simple abstinence from the act of generation will by no means deliver him from death: persons who have preserved their virginity die, and so, too, do castrates;[2] neither the former nor the latter enjoy even an especially long life. This is understandable. Death, speaking generally, is the disintegration of a being, the falling apart of its constituent factors. But it is the separation of the sexes—not eliminated by their external and transient union in the act of generation—it is this separation between male and female elements of the human being which is already in itself a state of disintegration, and the beginning of death. To remain divided into sexes means to remain on the path to death, and whoever either will not or cannot abandon this path is bound in accordance with natural necessity to follow it to the end. Whoever nourishes the root of death inevitably tastes the fruit of death. Only the human being in his entirety can be immortal, and if physical union cannot really restore the integrity of the human being, then this means that the spurious union must be replaced by a true one, but by no means by abstention from any union, i.e., by no means by the endeavor to preserve in *status quo* the divided, fallen apart and consequently mortal human nature.

In what then does the true union of the sexes consist, and how is it realized? Our life is so far removed from the truth in this relation that we accept as the norm here what is only the less extreme, the less crying abnormality. This needs to be elucidated more before we proceed farther.

II

In recent times in the psychiatric literature of Germany and France, several specialized books have appeared, devoted to what the author of one of them has termed *psychopathia sexualis*,[3] i.e., to various divergencies from the norm in sexual relations. Besides their specialist interest for jurists, medical men and the sufferers themselves, these treatises are also of interest from a perspective of which probably neither the authors themselves nor the majority of their readers ever thought. Especially in those treatises, written by scholars of repute, and presumably of irreproachable morals, we are astounded at the absence of any kind of clear and specific notion about the norm of sex relations, about what is requisite in this province and why it is so. As a consequence, the specification of deviations from the norm, i.e., the very subject of these studies, proves to be chosen fortuitously and arbitrarily. The customariness of a phenomenon, or the reverse, appears to be the sole criterion: those impulses and actions in the sexual domain which are comparatively rare are considered to be pathological deviations demanding treatment, while those which are customary and generally adopted are assumed to be the norm. Under this confusion of norm with customary deviation from it, the identification of what ought to be with what commonly occurs reaches at times the height of absurdity. Thus, in the case study section of one of these works we find under several reference numbers a repetition of the following therapeutic exercise: The patient is forced partly by persistent medical advice, but primarily by hypnotic suggestion, to occupy his imagination with the representation of a nude woman's body or other indecent pictures of a *normal*-sexual character (*sic*), and subsequently the treatment is recognized to have been successful and the convalescence complete if, under the influence of this artificial stimulation, the patient begins willingly, frequently and successfully to visit *lupanaria*. . . .[4] It is surprising that these respected scholars were not deterred, if only by the simple consideration that the more successful a cure of this kind is, the more easily may the patient be reduced to the necessity due to one medical specialty to turn for aid to another, so that the triumph of psychiatry may be the cause of great trouble to dermatology.

The perversions of sexual feeling studied in medical books are important for us, as being the extreme development of the same tendency which has made its way into the everyday usage of our society and is reckoned permissible and normal. These unusual phenomena represent only, in a more glaring aspect, the same disgrace which is inherent in our ordinary relations in this domain. It would be possible to prove this by a survey of all the particular aberrations of sexual feeling; but I hope that, in this matter, I may be forgiven for the incompleteness of my argument and may be allowed to confine myself to one more general and less repulsive anomaly in the province of sexual feeling. In many people, almost always of the male sex, this feeling is excited predominantly, and sometimes also exclusively, by one or another part in a being of the other sex (e.g., hair, a hand, a foot), and even by external objects—certain articles of attire and the like. This anomaly has received the appellation of fetishism in love. The abnormality of such fetishism consists, obviously, in the part being put in the place of the whole, the attribute in the place of the essence. But just as what excites the fetishist, the hair or the feet, are only parts of the woman's body, so this same body, in its whole structure, is only a part of the woman's being. Nevertheless the countless lovers of the woman's body, in and for itself, are not termed fetishists, do not acknowledge themselves to be insane and do not submit to treatment of any kind. In what however does the difference lie here? Can it be that the hand or the foot represents a lesser superficiality than the whole body?

If, in accordance with our principle, those sexual relations are abnormal in which the part is put in the place of the whole, then those people who in one way or another purchase a woman's body for the satisfaction of an emotional demand, and by doing so separate body from soul, must be acknowledged abnormal in sexual relations, psychologically ill persons, fetishists in love, or even necrophiles. But at present these lovers of what is spiritually dead, dying throughout their lives, are considered normal people, and through this living death almost the whole of humanity passes.

A conscience not deadened and an aesthetic feeling not hardened, in complete agreement with philosophic reasoning, condemn absolutely any sexual relations based upon the separation and isolation of the lower animal sphere in the human being from the higher ones. But apart from this principle it is impossible to find any solid criterion for the distinction between what is normal and what is abnormal in the domain of sex. If the demand for certain physiological acts possesses a right to satisfaction because it is a demand, come what may in consequence, then the demand of that "fetishist in love" possesses precisely the same claim to satisfaction, even if for him the single object desired in sexual relations turns out to be an apron, just washed and not yet dried, hanging on a clothes-line.[5] If also there is any difference discoverable between this eccentric and a regular frequenter of brothels, then of course the difference will be in favor of the fetishist. The attachment to a damp apron is natural and sincere beyond all doubt, for no kind of spurious motives for inventing it are possible, whereas many people frequent brothels, not in accordance with any real need, but out of false considerations of hygiene, in imitation of base examples, under the influence of drunkenness and so on.

People ordinarily condemn psychopathic manifestations of sexual feeling on the basis that they do not conform to the natural appointed end of the sexual act, namely propagation. To assert that a freshly washed apron, or even a worn-out shoe may serve for the production of posterity would, of course, be a paradox; but hardly less paradoxical would be the assumption that this end harmonizes with the institution of prostitutes. "Natural" depravity is obviously just as opposed to the generation of children as "unnatural," so that from this point of view also there is not the slightest basis to consider one of them normal and the other abnormal. If one, finally, takes the standpoint of harm to oneself and others, then, of course, the fetishist who cuts off locks of hair from ladies he does not know, or steals their handkerchiefs,[6] does harm to the property of others and to his own reputation, but is it possible to compare this harm with that caused by the unfortunate people who spread the terrible infection which is a sufficiently common consequence of the "natural" satisfactions of a "natural" demand?

III

All this I say not in justification of the unnatural, but in condemnation of the so-called natural means of satisfying sexual feeling. In general, when speaking of what is natural or unnatural, one ought not to forget that a human is a complex being, and that what is natural for one of his constituent principles or elements, may be unnatural for another, and consequently abnormal for a human as a whole.

For a human, *as an animal*, it is perfectly natural to allow unlimited satisfaction to his sexual demand, by means of a certain physical activity, but a human, as a moral being, finds this activity contrary to his higher nature and *is ashamed* of it. As a *social* animal, it is natural for a human to limit the physical function, which relates to other persons, by the demands of a social-moral *law*. This law extrinsically limits and conceals the animal function and makes it a means to a social end— the formation of a family union. But the essence of the matter is not changed by this. Family union is based all the same on the external material union of the sexes: it leaves the animal-human in his former disintegrated, halved state, which of necessity leads to the further disintegration of the human being, i.e., to death.

If a human, over and above his animal nature, were only a social-moral being, then of these two antagonistic elements—which are equally natural for him—the ultimate triumph would remain with the first. The social-moral law and its basic objectification—the family— lead a human being's animal nature within the limits necessary for generic progress; they regulate mortal life, but they do not reveal the path to immortality. The individual being, in the social-moral order of existence, likewise wears itself out and dies, just as if it had remained exclusively under the law of animal life. The elephant and the raven prove to be significantly longer-lived than even the most punctiliously virtuous human.[7] But in humans, besides the animal nature and the so-cial-moral law, there is yet a third loftier principle—the spiritual, mystical or divine. Here also, in the realm of love and of sexual relations, it is that "stone which the builders refused," and it "is become the head stone of the corner."[8] Before the physical union in animal nature, which leads to death, and before the legal union in the social-moral order, which does not save one from death, there ought to be the union in God, which leads to immortality because it does not merely limit the mortal life of nature by the law of humans, but regenerates it by the eternal and imperishable power of grace. This third element—the first in the true order—with the demands inherent in it, is wholly *natural* to a human in his entirety, as a being partaking in the supreme divine principle and forming a link between it and the world. But the two lower elements—animal nature and social law—likewise natural in their proper place, become *unnatural* when they are taken apart from what is higher and relied upon in place of it. In the province of sexual love it is not only *any* disordered satisfaction of emo-tional demands, devoid of higher spiritual consecration after the fashion of the lower animals, which is unnatu-ral for humans (not to mention various monstrous phenomena of sexual psychopathy). Equally unnatural and unworthy of humans are those unions between people of different sexes which are entered into and kept up *only* on the basis of civil law, exclusively for moral-social ends, with neglect or inactivity of the properly spiritual, mystical principle in humans. But from the point of view of the entire human being, just such an unnatural rearrangement of all true relations prevails in our life and is acknowledged as normal, so that all condemnation is transferred from it to the unfortunate psychopaths of love, who only take to excesses which are ludicrous, disgraceful and sometimes repulsive, but for the most part comparatively harmless, this most commonly accepted and prevalent perversion.

IV

Those manifold perversions of the sexual instinct to which psychiatrists devote their attention are only unusual variations of a general and all-pervading perversion of these relations in humanity—that perversion by which the kingdom of sin and death is maintained and perpetuated. Though there are three relations or bonds between the sexes, all natural to a human in his entirety, i.e., the bond of animal existence in accordance with lower nature; secondly the moral-earthly bond, subject to law; and lastly the bond of spiritual life or of union in God—though all these relations exist in humanity, yet they are realized in unnatural ways, especially when separated one from another, in the reverse of their true meaning and order of succession, and out of due proportion.

In the first place in our reality appears what ought truly to be in the last—the animal physical bond. It is recognized as the basis of the whole matter, whereas it ought to be only its final culmination. For many humans here the basis coincides with the culmination; they do not go further than animal relations. For others, the social, moral structure of a legitimate family union is raised on this broad basis. Here the earthly center is accepted as the summit of life, and what ought to serve as a free, intelligent expression in the temporal process of an eternal union, becomes the forced channel of a meaningless material life. And then, finally, as a rare and exclusive phenomenon, there remains for an elect few a pure spiritual love, from which all real content has been removed beforehand by other inferior bonds, so that it is obliged to be satisfied with a visionary and fruitless sentimentality, without any real task or end in life. This unfortunate spiritual love reminds one of the little angels in old paintings, which have only a head, then wings and nothing more. These angels do nothing for want of hands, and cannot move forward, seeing that there is only power enough in their wings to support them motionless at a certain height. In such an elevated, but extremely unsatisfactory, situation is spiritual love found to be. Physical passion has before it a certain task, though it is a shameful one; a legitimate family union likewise accomplishes a task, still necessary, though it is also of mediocre worth. But spiritual love, as it is manifested hitherto, has, so far as is known, no task of any kind at all, and therefore it is not surprising that the majority of practical people "don't believe in love, or take it to be poetry."

This exclusively spiritual love is quite obviously as much an anomaly as an exclusively physical love and as an exclusively earthly union. The absolute norm is the restoration of the integrity of the human being, and if this norm is infringed, in either one direction or another, the result in every case is that an abnormal, unnatural phenomenon arises. So-called spiritual love is a phenomenon which is not only abnormal, but also completely purposeless, because the separation of the spiritual from the sensuous, to which such love aspires, is accomplished without it, and in the best possible way, by death. True spiritual love is not a feeble imitation and anticipation of death, but a triumph over death, not a separation of the immortal from the mortal, of the eternal from the temporal, but a transfiguration of the mortal into the immortal, the acceptance of the temporal into the eternal. False spirituality is a denial of the flesh; true spirituality is the regeneration of the flesh, its salvation, its resurrection from the dead.

V

"So God created man in His own image, in the image of God created He him; male and female created He them."[9]

"This is a great mystery, but I speak concerning Christ and the church."[10]

Not to any separate portion of the human being, but to the true unity of its two basic sides, the male and the female, is ascribed originally the mysterious Divine image, in accordance with which man was created. As God is in relation to His creation, as Christ is in relation to His Church, so the husband ought to be in relation to his wife. Although these words are generally known, their meaning is little understood. As God creates the universe, as Christ is the builder of the Church, so the man ought to create and build his female complement. That the male represents the active and the female the passive principle, that the former ought to exert an educational influence over the character and mind of the latter—these, of course, are elementary propositions. But we have in view not this superficial relation, but that "great mystery" of which the apostle speaks. This great mystery represents an essential analogy, though not an identity, between the human relation and the Divine. Now the building of the Church by Christ is distinguished from the creation of the universe by God, as such. God created the universe out of nothing, i.e., out of the pure potentiality of being, or out of emptiness, subsequently fulfilled, i.e., receiving from the Divine activity real forms of things which are conceived mentally. Christ however builds up the Church out of matter already manifestly formed, animated and in its own parts self-acting, to which only a principle of new spiritual life in a new higher sphere of unity needed to be imparted. Finally, man for his creative activity possesses, in the person of a woman, material equal to himself in the degree of its actualization, before whom he enjoys only the potential pre-eminence of initiative, only the right and the obligation to take the first step on the road to perfection, but no pre-eminence in the actual accomplishment of perfection. God is in relation to creation as the all to the nothing, i.e., as the absolute fulness of being to the pure potentiality of being. Christ is in relation to the Church as actual perfection to the potentiality of perfection being formed into real perfection. The relation between husband and wife is the relation between two differently acting, yet equally imperfect potentialities, which attain perfection only in the process of reciprocity. In other words, God receives nothing from creation for Himself, i.e., no kind of increase, but gives everything to it. Christ receives from the Church no increase at all in the sense of perfection, and gives all perfection to her, but He does receive from the Church an increase in the sense of the fulness of His collective body. Finally, man and his female *alter ego* mutually fulfill each other, not only in the real but also in the ideal sense, attaining perfection only through reciprocity. Man can restore formatively the image of God in the living object of his love, only when at the same time he also restores that image in himself. However, he does not possess the power for this in himself, for if he possessed it he would not stand in need of restoration; and as he does not possess it in himself, he is obliged to receive it from God. Consequently, the man (husband) is the creative, formative principle, its author and source as regards his female complement, not in and for himself, but as the intermediary or channel of the Divine power. Strictly speaking, Christ also does not build by some sort of His own separate power, but by that same creative power of the Godhead; yet being Himself God, He possesses this power by nature and *in actu,* while we have power by grace and adoption, possessing in ourselves only the possibility (potential) to receive it.

When I pass on to the exposition of the basic moments in the process of the realization of true love, i.e., in the process of the integration of the human being, or the restoration in him of the Divine image, I foresee the perplexity I shall cause to many. Why, say they, do you climb to such inaccessible and fantastic heights over such a simple thing as love? If I had considered the religious norm of love fantastic, then I should not of course have propounded it. In exactly the same way, if I had had in view only *simple* love, i.e., the ordinary, commonplace relations between the sexes—that which actually exists, and not that which ought to be—then of course I would have refrained from all discussion of this subject, because undoubtedly these simple relations belong to those things about which someone has said: it's not nice to do it, but it is even worse to talk about it. But love, as I understand it, is, on the contrary, an extraordinarily complex affair, obscure and intricate, demanding fully conscious analysis and investigation, in which one needs to be concerned not about simplicity, but about the truth. . . . A rotten stump is, undoubtedly, simpler than a many-branched tree, and a corpse is simpler than a living human. The simple relation to love is completed by that definitive and ultimate simplification which is termed death. Such an inevitable and unsatisfactory end of "simple" love impels us to seek for another, more complex principle.

VI

The matter of true love is above all based on *faith*. The root meaning of love, as has already been shown, consists in the acknowledgment of absolute significance for another being. But this being in its empirical being, as the subject of real sensuous perception, does not have absolute significance: it is imperfect in its worth and transient as to its existence. Consequently, we can assert absolute significance for it only by faith, which is the assurance of things hoped for, the conviction of things not seen. But to what does faith relate in the present instance? What does it strictly mean to believe in the absolute, and, what is the same thing, everlasting significance of this individual person? To assert that he himself, as such, in his particularity and separateness, possesses absolute significance would be as absurd as it is blasphemous. Of course the word "worship" is very generally used in the sphere of amorous relations, but then the word "madness" likewise possesses its legitimate application in this domain. So then, observing the law of logic, which does not allow us to admit contradictory definitions, and likewise obeying the command of true religion, which forbids the worship of idols, we must, by faith in the object of our love, understand the affirmation of this object as it exists in God, and as in this sense possessing everlasting significance. It must be understood that this transcendental relation to one's other, this mental transference of it into the sphere of the Divine, presupposes the same relation to oneself, the same transference and affirmation of oneself in the sphere of the absolute. I can only acknowledge the absolute significance of a given person, or believe in him (without which true love is impossible), by affirming him in God, and consequently by belief in God Himself, and in myself, as possessing in God the center and root of my own existence. This triune faith is already a certain internal act, and by this act is laid the first basis of a true union of the man with his other and the restoration in it (or in them) of the image of the triune God. The act of faith, under the real conditions of time and place, is a prayer (in the basic, not in the technical sense of the word). The indivisible union of oneself and another in this relation is the first step towards a real union. In itself this step is small, but without it nothing more advanced or greater is possible.

Seeing that for God, the eternal and indivisible, all is together and at once, all is in one, then to affirm any individual being whatsoever in God signifies to affirm him not in his separateness but in the all, or more accurately—in the unity of the all. But seeing that this individual being, in his given reality, does not enter into the unity of the all, but exists separately as an individualized material phenomenon, then the object of our believing love is necessarily to be distingished from the empirical object of our instinctive love, though it is also inseparably bound up with it. It is one and the same person in two distinguishable aspects, or in two different spheres of being—the ideal and the real. The first is as yet only an idea. By steadfast, believing and insightful love, however, we know that this idea is not an arbitrary fiction of our own, but that it expresses the *truth* of the object, only a truth as yet not realized in the sphere of external, real phenomena.

This true idea of the beloved object, though it shines through the real phenomenon in the instant of love's intense emotion, is at first manifested in a clearer aspect only as the object of imagination. The concrete form of this imagination, the ideal image in which I clothe the beloved person at the given moment, is of course created by me, but it is not created out of nothing. And the subjectivity of this image as such, i.e., as it manifests itself here and now before the eyes of my soul, by no means proves that it is subjective, i.e., a characteristic of an imaginary object which exists for me alone. If for me, who am myself on this side of the transcendental world, a certain ideal object appears to be only the product of my own imagination, this does not interfere with its full reality in another higher sphere of being. And though our real life is outside this higher sphere, yet our mind is not wholly alien to it, and we can possess a certain abstract comprehension of the laws of its being. And here is the first and basic law: If in our world separate and isolated existence is a fact and an actuality, while unity is only a concept and an idea, then in the higher sphere, on the contrary, reality appertains to the unity, or more accurately, to the unity-of-the-all, while separateness and individualization exist only potentially and subjectively.

From this it follows that the being of *this* person in the transcendental sphere is not an individual one, in the sense of a real being in this world. There, i.e., in the truth, the individual person is only a living and real yet indivisible ray of one ideal light—the unity-of-the-all essence. This ideal person, or personified idea, is only an individualization of the unity-of-the-all, which is indivisibly present in each of its individualizations. So, when we imagine the ideal form of the beloved object, then under this form is communicated to us this same unity-of-the-all essence. How then are we to think of it?

VII

God, as one, distinguishing from Himself His other, i.e., all that is not He, unites this all with Himself, presenting it to Himself, all together and all at once, in an absolutely perfect form, and, consequently, as a unity. This *other* unity, distinct though not separable from the primordial Divine unity, is, relative to God, a passive, feminine unity, seeing that here the eternal emptiness (pure potentiality) receives the fulness of the Divine existence. But if *at the basis* of this eternal femininity lies pure nothing, then for God this nothing is eternally hidden by the image of the absolute perfection which is being received from the Divinity. This perfection, which for us is still only being realized, is for God, i.e., in the truth, already real. That ideal unity towards which our world is aspiring, and which constitutes the end of the cosmic and historical process, cannot be only some-one's subjective understanding (for whose, pray, is it?); truly it is like the external object of Divine love, like His eternal other.

This living ideal of the Divine love, antecedent to our love, contains in itself the secret of the idealization of our love. In it the idealization of the lower being exists together with an incipient realization of the higher, and in this is the truth of love's intense emotion. Complete realization, the transformation of the individual feminine being into the ray of the eternal Divine femininity, inseparable from its resplendent source, will be a real, not merely subjective but also objective, reunion of the individual human being with God, the restoration in him of the living and immortal Divine image.

The object of true love is not simple, but twofold. We love, in the first place, the ideal being (ideal not in the abstract sense, but in the sense of belonging to another higher sphere of being), the being whom we ought to install in our ideal world. And, in the second place, we love the natural human being, who furnishes the living personal material for the realization of the former, and who is idealized by means of it, not in the sense of our subjective imagination, but in the sense of its actual objective transformation or regeneration. In this way true love is both *ascending* and *descending (amor ascendens et amor descendens)*, or it is those two Aphrodites whom Plato excellently distinguished, but separated poorly—Αφροδιτη Ουρανια and Αφροδιτη πανδημος).[11] For God, His *other* (i.e., the universe) possesses from all eternity the image of perfect femininity, but He desires that this image should exist not merely for Him, but that it should be realized and incarnated in each individual being capable of union with it. Such a realization and incarnation is also the aspiration of the eternal Femininity itself, which is not merely an inert image in the Divine mind, but a living spiritual being possessed of all the fulness of powers and activities. The whole process of the cosmos and of history is the process of its realization and incarnation in a great manifold of forms and degrees.

In sexual love, truly understood and truly realized, this Divine essence receives the means for its definitive, ultimate incarnation in the individual life of a human, the means of the most profound and at the same time the most external and real-perceptible union with it. Hence come those beams of an unearthly bliss, of a breath of gladness not of this world, by which love even when imperfect is accompanied, and which make it, even when imperfect, the highest delight of men and gods—*hominum divomque voluptas*.[12] Hence also the profound suffering of love, powerless to hold fast its true object, and ever withdrawing farther and farther from it.

Hence also is derived the legitimate place of that element of adoration and boundless devotion which is so peculiar to love, yet possesses so little meaning if it relates only to the earthly object, in separation from the heavenly one.

The mystical basis of the twofold, or, to speak more accurately, of the two-sided character of love, determines the question of the possibility of a repetition of love. The heavenly object of our love is only one, always and for all humans one and the same—the eternal Divine Femininity. But seeing that the task of true love consists not in merely doing homage to this supreme object, but in realizing and incarnating it in another lower being of the same feminine form, though of an earthly nature, and seeing that this being is only one of many, then its unique significance for the lover of course *may* also be transient. But *it ought to be* unique and for this reason is decided in each individual case and depends not on one single and unchangeable mystical basis of the true process of love, but on its remotest moral and physical conditions; and into these we ought also to inquire.

1. [Dionysus is, of course, the god of fertility. Hades as the ruler of the underworld is traditionally associated with death. There was, however, a tradition within which chtonian gods came to be associated with their opposites. This explains how Hades could simultaneously represent death and fertility.]

2. [The castrates (Russian "skoptsy") are known already in classical mythology. Considered heretics by the Russian Orthodox Church, groups of these individuals were still in existence in nineteenth century Russia.]

3. [Alfred Binet, the French psychologist (1857–1911), published his article "Le fétichisme dans l'amour" in the *Revue philosophique*, XIV (1887), pp. 142–167, 252–275. Richard Baron von Krafft-Ebing, a physician and Professor of Psychiatry at the University of Vienna (1840–1902), published his celebrated *Psychopathia sexualis* in Stuttgart in 1886. In spite of the fact that the work was written in Latin, it became a heated topic of discussion throughout Europe.]

4. [Solovyov chooses the Latin word for "brothels" perhaps influenced by the Latin version of *Psychopathia sexualis*.]

5. Cf. Binet "Le fétichisme en amour"; likewise Krafft-Ebing, *Psychopathia sexualis*. [See Cases 35 and 108 in *Psychopathia*.]

6. [See Case 110].

7. As regards recent discussions about death and the dread of death, it must be remarked that besides dread and indifference—equally unworthy of a reflective and loving being—there is also a third relation—the struggle against and triumph over death. What matters is not one's own death, about which morally and physically healthy people, of course, trouble little, but the death of others, those whom we love, towards whom an impartial relation is for the lover impossible. (Cf. John 11: 33–36.)

   Resignation in this respect would be a demand of reason in the latter case, only if a human's death would be the absolutely inevitable outcome. But people always only surmise this and never try to prove it, and not without cause, for to prove it is impossible. That *under certain conditions* death is necessary, about this of course there is no dispute: but that these conditions are the only possible ones, that it is impossible to change them, and that consequently death is an *absolute* necessity—for this there is not a shadow of rational basis.

8. [Psalms 118:22.]

9. [Genesis 1:27.]

10. [Paul. Ephesians 5:32.]

11. [Plato in the *Symposium* 180D,E distinguishes between Aphrodite Ourania (the heavenly or spiritual) and Aphrodite Pandemos (the earthly or human Venus).]

12. [Lucretius, "On the Nature of Things." "the desire of men and gods."]

CHAPTER 5

I

Involuntary and immediate feeling reveals to us the meaning of love as the highest manifestation of individual life, which finds in union with another being its own proper infinity. Is not this momentary revelation sufficient? Is it perhaps a small thing to really experience at least once in a lifetime one's own absolute significance?

> And I know, having gazed at times upon the stars,
> that we looked on them as gods, you and I.[1]

This is hardly sufficient, even for a poetic feeling, but *consciousness of the truth* and the *will to life* decidedly cannot be reconciled on this basis. An infinity which is only *momentary* is a contradiction unendurable for the mind, a bliss which is only in the past is suffering for the will. They are those beams of another world, after which

> Yet darker is the gloom of everyday existence,
> As after a brilliant autumnal lightning.[2]

97

If such moments are only an illusion, then in remembrance they can evoke only shame and the bitterness of disenchantment; but if they were not an illusion, if they have revealed to us a certain reality, which afterwards disappeared and was hidden from us, then why should we reconcile ourselves to this disappearance? If what is lost was true, then the task of consciousness and of the will lies not in accepting the loss as final, but in understanding and removing its causes.

The proximate cause (as was partially shown in the preceding chapter) consists in the distortion of the very relation of love itself. It begins very early: hardly does the primordial intense emotion of love succeed in showing us a region of another, better reality—with another principle and law of life—than we straightaway strive to avail ourselves of the rise in energy which is the consequence of this revelation, not to advance farther whither it summons us, but only to take root more firmly and to become settled more steadfastly in that former base reality, above which love had just raised us. Good tidings from a lost paradise—tidings of the possibility of its recovery—we accept as an invitation to become finally *naturalized* in earthly exile, to enter without delay into full and hereditary possession of our own minute portion, with all its thistles and briars. That breach of personal limitedness, which is the index of the passion of love and constitutes its basic meaning, leads in deed only to a *twofold egoism*, and then to a threefold and so on. Of course, this is anyhow better than the egoism of one living in isolation; but the dawn of love has revealed to us completely different horizons.

As soon as the life-sphere of the union of love is transferred to material reality, as it is, then at once the order itself of the union is distorted in a corresponding manner. Its "not-of-this-world" mystical basis, which so powerfully made itself known in primordial passion, is forgotten as a passing exaltation, while the most desirable material end, which ought to be merely the ultimate conditioned manifestation, is recognized as the primary condition of love. This latter—putting the physical union in the primary place and bereaving it in that way of its *human* meaning, reducing it to its animal meaning—makes love not only powerless against death, but itself inevitably becomes the moral grave of love long before the physical grave takes the lovers.

Direct personal resistance to such an order of things is more difficult of accomplishment than of comprehension: it is possible to indicate it in a few words. To abrogate this base order among the manifestations of life, it is necessary above all to acknowledge it as abnormal, asserting thereby that there exists another, normal order, in which all that is external and incidental is subordinated to the internal meaning of life. Such an assertion ought not to be merely verbal; to the experience of external feelings ought to be opposed not an abstract principle, but another experience—*the experience of faith*. This latter is incomparably more difficult than the former, for it is dependent more on internal

99

action than on reception from without. Only by consistent acts of conscious faith do we enter into real correspondence with the realm of the truly-existent, and through it into true correlation with our "other." Only on this basis can we retain and strengthen in consciousness that absoluteness for us of another person (and consequently also the absoluteness of our union with him) which is immediately and unaccountably revealed in the intense emotion of love, for this emotion of love comes and passes away, but the faith of love abides.

But, in order for the faith to be a living faith, it must set itself steadfastly against that existing society where meaningless chance builds its dominion upon the play of animal passions and, still worse, human passions. Against these hostile powers, believing faith has only one defensive weapon—endurance to the end. To earn its bliss, it must take up its cross. In our materialistic society it is impossible to preserve true love, unless we understand and accept it as a moral achievement. Not without reason does the Orthodox Church in her *marriage* ceremony make mention of holy *martyrs* and compare their crowns to the bridal crowns.

Religious faith and moral achievement safeguard an individual human and his love from being engulfed by materialistic society during his lifetime, but they do not give him a triumph over death. Internal regeneration of the feeling of love and the amendment of distorted relations of love do not amend or change the basic law of physical life, either in the external world or in the human himself. He remains *in reality* as before a limited being, subject to material nature. His internal—mystical and moral—union with his complementary individuality cannot overcome either their mutual separateness and impenetrability or their common dependence upon the material world. The last word remains not with the moral achievement, but with the inexorable law of organic life and death, and men who stand up to the end in defense of the eternal ideal die with human dignity but with the powerlessness of the animal.

So long as the individual's achievement is confined to its proximate object—the amendment of the distorted personal relation between two beings—it remains of necessity without final success and is limited to this its own immediate concern. For the evil with which true love comes into collision, the evil of material separateness and impenetrability, and of the external resistance of two beings who internally fulfill one another—this evil is a particular yet typical instance of the general distortion to which our life is subject, and not ours alone, but the life of the whole world.

An individual can really be saved, i.e., can regenerate and immortalize his individual life in true love, only conjointly or together with all others. He possesses the right and the obligation to defend his individuality from the basic law of general existence, but not to separate his own welfare from the true welfare of all living beings. From the fact that the deepest and most intense manifestation of love is expressed in the mutual relation of two beings who fulfill each other, it by no means follows that this mutual relation can separate and isolate itself from all the rest, as something self-sufficient. On the contrary, such isolation is the death of love, for in itself the sexual relation, in spite of all its subjective significance, proves (objectively) to be only a transient empirical phenomenon. In just the same way, from the fact that the perfected union of two such single beings will always remain the true and fundamental form of individual life, it does not at all follow that, when this life-form sets its keystone in its individual perfection, it is bound to remain empty, since, on the contrary, by the very nature of the human being, it is capable and predestined to be filled with the universal content. Finally, if the moral meaning of love demands the reunion of that which is wrongfully separated, demands the identification of oneself with another, then to separate the problem of our individual perfection from the process of worldwide unification would be contrary to this same moral meaning of love, even if such a separation were physically possible.

II

Thus any attempt to exclude and isolate the individual process of regeneration in true love meets with a threefold insurmountable obstacle. The fact is, our indi-

vidual life with its love, when separated from the process of universal life, inevitably proves to be, firstly
physically groundless and powerless against time and
death, secondly intellectually empty and lacking in content, and finally morally unworthy. If fantasy overleaps
the physical and logical obstacles, then it is bound to
come to a standstill before the moral impossibility.

Let us suppose something completely fantastic—let
us suppose that some human has so strengthened his
spirit by consistent concentration of will and consciousness, and so purified his bodily nature by ascetic
achievement, that he has really restored (for himself and
for his complementary "other") the true integrity of
human individuality, has attained complete spiritualization and immortality. Will this regenerate individuality
take any delight in its lonely bliss, in that society where
everyone as before endures pain and dies? But let us go
still farther. Let us suppose that this regenerate pair has
received the capacity to communicate to all the rest its
own superior condition. This, of course, is impossible
inasmuch as it is dependent on personal moral achievement, but let there be something in the nature of a
philosopher's stone[3] or an elixir of life. Then every
living thing on earth would recover from its evils and
maladies, would be free and immortal. But in order that
they may be at the same time happy, one more condition is necessary: they must forget their parents, forget
the actual authors of this new prosperity, because no
matter what fantastic significance could be ascribed to a

personal achievement, it would still be necessary that thousands and thousands of generations, by their united collective effort, should create that culture, those moral and intellectual structures, without which the task of individual regeneration could not be accomplished, or even conceived. And these billions of people, who gave their lives for others, will rot in their graves, while their idle posterity will unconcernedly enjoy their gratuitous happiness! But this would presuppose moral misanthropy and yet worse, because even savages revere their ancestors and maintain contact with them. In what way can the ultimate and highest state of humanity be based upon injustice, ingratitude and forgetfulness? A human being, having attained the highest perfection, cannot accept such an unmerited gift; if he is not in a condition to snatch away from Death *all* its prey, it is better that he should renounce immortality.

"Shatter this goblet, in it poison lies."

By good fortune all this is merely arbitrary and idle fantasy, for the matter never comes to such a tragic test of *moral* solidarity in humanity, by power of our *natural* solidarity with the whole world—by power of the physical impossibility of the *individual* solution of the task of existence by a single human being or by a single generation. Our regeneration is indissolubly bound up with the regeneration of the universe and with the transfiguration of its forms of space and time. The true life of individuality, in its full and absolute significance, is accomplished and perpetuated only in the corresponding development of the life of the universe, in which we can and ought to take an active part, but which is not created by us. Our personal concern, so far as it is true, is a common concern of the whole world—the realization and individualization of the unity-of-the-all idea and the spiritualization of matter. It is prepared by the cosmic process in the world of nature, and is continued and completed by the historical process in humanity. Our *ignorance* about the interconnecting bond of concrete particulars in the unity of the whole leaves us, notwithstanding, freedom of action, which, with all its consequences, has already entered from all eternity into the absolute and all-embracing design.

The idea of unity-of-the-all can finally be realized or embodied only in the fulness of completed individualities; this means that the final end of the whole matter is the higher development of each individuality in the fullest unity of all, but this end necessarily includes also our own life's end, which consequently is not isolated or separated by any consideration or possibility from the end common to all. We are just as necessary to the world as the world is to us. The universe from time immemorial has been interested in the preservation, development and perpetuation of all that is really necessary and desirable for us, all that is positive and of worth in our individuality. And it remains to us only to accept, if possible more consciously and actively, our share in the general historical process—for our own selves and for all others *inseparably*.

III

True being, or the idea of unity-of-the-all, is opposed in our world by material existence, which, with its senseless stubbornness, stifles even our love, and does not allow its meaning to be realized. The essential characteristic of this material existence is a *twofold impenetrability*:

(1) Impenetrability in *time,* by power of which every successive moment of existence does not preserve the preceding one within itself, but excludes it or dislodges it from existence, so that each new thing in the sphere of matter originates at the expense of, or to the detriment of, what preceded it.

(2) Impenetrability in *space,* by power of which two parts of matter (two bodies) cannot at the same time occupy one and the same place, i.e., one and the same part of space, but necessarily dislodge one another.

In this way, that which lies at the basis of our world is being in a state of disintegration, being dismembered into parts and moments which exclude one another. We are bound to accept such deep soil and such a broad basis for this fatal separateness of beings, which causes all the misery of our personal lives. To overcome this twofold impenetrability of bodies and phenomena, to make the real external medium conformable to the inner unity-of-the-all idea—there is the task of the process of the world, as simple in general conception as it is complex and difficult in concrete realization.

The predominance of the material basis of our world and of life is still so great that many people, even those with conscientious but somewhat one-sided minds, think that in general nothing exists apart from this material existence in its various modifications. However, it goes without saying that the acknowledgment of this visible world as the only one is an arbitrary hypothesis, which is possible to believe, but impossible to prove. And even if we do not go beyond the limits of this world or the point of view of facts, we are forced to acknowledge that materialism is wrong all the same. It is a fact (and in our visible world there are many such) that not only is there a modification of material existence in its spatial and temporal impenetrability, but there is even a direct negation and abrogation of this same impenetrability. Such, in the first place, is the general *gravitational pull*, by which parts of the material world do not exclude one another, but, on the contrary, aspire mutually to include one another and to mingle with each other. For the sake of a preconceived principle it is possible to erect so-called scientific hypotheses one on top of another, but for a rational intelligence such hypotheses based upon specifications of inert matter will never succeed in explaining factors of a directly contradictory character; they will never succeed in deriving attraction from repulsion, in extracting attraction from impenetrability—or in understanding aspiration as inertia. Meanwhile, without these immaterial factors even the simplest bodily existence would be impossible. Matter itself in itself, of course, is only this unspecified and disconnected conglomeration of atoms, to which, with more generosity than solid basis, movement is subjoined as if it were inherent in it. In any event, for the specific and permanent union of material particles into bodies, it is necessary that their impenetrability, or what is the same thing their absolute disconnectedness, should be transmuted into a greater or less degree of positive co-operation among them. In this way also, all our universe, insofar as it is not a chaos of discrete atoms but a single and united whole, presupposes, over and above its fragmentary material, a form of unity, and likewise an active power subduing to this unity elements antagonistic to it. The unity of the material world is not a material unity—such in general there cannot be; it is a *contradictio in adjecto*. Organized by the law of gravity, which is contrary-to-matter (and this, from the point of view of materialism, means contrary-to-what-is-natural), the body of the universe is the totality of the real-ideal, the psycho-physical, or simply (in direct agreement with the idea of Newton about the *sensorium Dei*) it is a *mystical body*.[4]

Besides the worldwide force of gravity, the ideal unity-of-the-all is realized in a spiritual-corporeal fashion in the world-body by means of light and other kindred phenomena (electricity, magnetism, heat). The character of these is found to be in such startling contrast to the properties of impenetrable and inert matter that even materialistic science is constrained by the evidence to acknowledge in them a special kind of half-material substance which it terms aether. This is imponderable matter, impenetrable and all-penetrating—in a word it is *immaterial matter*.

By these embodiments of the unity-of-the-all idea—gravity and aether—our real world is held together, and matter in itself, i.e., the dead conglomeration of inert and impenetrable atoms, is only conceived by abstracting intelligence, but is not observed or revealed in any such actuality. We know of no moment when genuine reality would appertain to the material chaos and the idea of the cosmos would be a disembodied and powerless shade; we only assume such a moment as a starting point of the world process, within the limits of our visible universe.

Already also in the natural world everything appertains to the idea, but the true essence of the latter demands not only that everything should belong to it, that everything should be included in it, but also *that the idea itself should belong to everything*, that everything, i.e., *all* particular and individual beings, and consequently *each one* of them, should really be possessed of the ideal unity-of-the-all, should comprise it in itself. Perfect unity-of-the-all, in accordance with its own conception of itself, demands complete equilibrium, equivalence and equality of right between the one and the all, between the whole and the parts, between the general and the particular. The fulness of the idea demands that the greatest possible unity of the whole should be realized in the greatest possible independence and freedom of the particular and single elements—in them themselves, through them, and for them. In this direction the cosmic process attains to the creation of animal individuality, for which the unity of the idea exists in the image of the *species* and is felt in its full power in the moment of sexual attraction, when the inward unity or community with the other, with the "all," receives its concrete embodiment in the relation to a single person of the other sex, who represents in itself this complementary "all" in one. The same individual life of the living organism already contains in itself a certain, though limited, likeness of the unity-of-the-all, inasmuch as in it is realized a complete solidarity and reciprocity of all the particular organs and elements in the unity of the living body. But as this organic solidarity *in* the animal does not reach beyond the limits of its bodily structure, so also *for* it the image of the complementary "other" is wholly limited to such a single body with the possibility only of a material and partial union. Therefore the supratemporal infinity or eternity of the idea, operating in the living creative power of love, assumes here the base, rectilineal form of limitless propagation, i.e., the repetition of one and the same organism in the monotonous replacement of single temporal existences.

In human life the direct line of propagation of the species, though it is preserved in the main, yet (thanks to the development of consciousness and conscious interchange) reappears in the historical process in ever wider circles of social and cultural organisms. These social organisms are produced by that same living creative power of love which gives birth to physical organisms. This power directly creates the family, and the family is the formative element of every community. In spite of this genetic bond, the relation of the human individuality to the community is essentially different from the relation of the animal individuality to the species: the human is not a transient exemplar of the community. The unity of the social organism is *really co-existent* with each one of its individual members; it possesses being not only in him and through him, but also *for* him, and is found in a specific bond and correlation with him: communal and individual life mutually penetrate each other in all directions. Consequently, we possess here a far more perfect image of the embodiment of the unity-of-the-all idea, than in the physical organism. Moreover, here begins from within (out of the consciousness) the process of integration in time (or *in contrast to* time). The persistent succession of the generations of humanity notwithstanding, the first principles of the immortalization of individuality are already there in the religion of our forefathers—that basis of all culture—in tradition, in the memory of the community, in art, and finally in the science of history. The imperfect, rudimentary character of such immortalization corresponds to the imperfection of human individuality itself and to that of the community. But the progress is indubitable, and the ultimate task is becoming clearer and closer at hand.

IV

If the root of false existence consists in impenetrability, i.e., in the mutual exclusion of beings by each other, then true life is to live in another as in oneself, or to find in another the positive and absolute fulfillment of one's own being. The basis and type of this true life remains and always will remain sexual or conjugal love. But a proper realization of it is, as we have seen, impossible, without a corresponding transformation of all outward conditions; i.e., the integration of individual life necessarily demands the same integration in the spheres of communal and universal life. Specific discrimination, or separableness of spheres of life, collective as well as individual, never will be, and ought not to be, abrogated, since such a general fusion would lead to uniformity and emptiness, and not to fulness of being. True union presupposes the true separateness of those being united, i.e., a separateness by power of which they do not exclude, but mutually replenish each other, each finding in the other the fulness of his own proper life. As in the love of two individual beings, diverse but enjoying equal rights and of equal worth, each serves the other, not as a negative limitation but as positive fulfillment, so in precisely the same way it must also be in all spheres of collective life; every social organism ought to be for each of its members not an external limit of his activity, but a positive support and fulfillment. As for sexual love (in the sphere of personal existence), the single "other" is at the same time all, so, on its side, the social *all*, by power of the positive solidarity of all its elements, ought to manifest itself for each of them as a real unity, as the other living being which would fulfill him in a new and wider sphere.

If the relation of the individual members of a community to one another ought to be brotherly (or filial—in accordance with their relation to past generations and to their social representatives), then their bond with the whole of their common spheres—the local, the national and finally the universal—ought to be still more internal, all-inclusive and significant. This bond between the living human source (personal) and the unity-of-the-all idea incarnated in the social spiritual-physical organism, ought to be a living *syzygetic* relation.[5] It ought not to be subjected to its communal sphere or to dominate it, but to be in loving reciprocity with it, to serve as its active fertilizing source of motion and to find in it the fulness of life's conditions and possibilities—such is the relation of the true human individuality, not only to its immediate social environment and to its nation, but also to the whole of humanity.

In the Bible, cities, nations, the people of Israel and, later, also all regenerate humanity, or the universal Church, are represented in the image of a female individuality, and this is not a simple metaphor. From the fact that the image of the unity of social bodies is not perceptible to our external feelings, it by no means follows that it does not exist at all: you know also that our own bodily image is not altogether to be perceived and is invisible to an isolated brain cell and to a globule of blood. And if we as individualities, capable of fulness of being, are distinguished from these elementary individualities not only by greater clearness and range of intellectual knowledge, but also by greater power of creative imagination, then I see no need to disclaim this superiority. As it would not be either with an image or without an image, it is requisite above all that we should have a relation to social and worldwide circles as to a real living being, with which we (never merging into inseparability) are in the closest and fullest reciprocal action. Such an extension of the syzygetic relation over spheres of collective and universal being perfects the individuality itself, communicating to it unity and fulness of life's content, and thereby elevates and makes immortal the fundamental individual form of love.

It is beyond question that the historical process is being perfected in this direction, gradually destroying false or insufficient forms of unions among human beings (patriarchal, despotic and one-sidedly individualist), and at the same time approximating ever more and more not only to the unification of all humanity in the solidarity of the whole, but also to the establishment of a true syzygetic image of this oneness of all humanity. In proportion as the unity-of-the-all idea is actually realized through the strengthening and perfecting of its individual human elements, the forms of false separation, or of the impenetrability of beings in space and time, necessarily grow feeble and disappear. But for their complete abrogation and for the final immortalization of all individualities, not only those now living but also those of time past, it is necessary that the process of integration should pass beyond the limits of social or specifically human life and should include within itself the sphere of the cosmos from which it proceeded. In the ordering of the physical world (the cosmic process), the Divine idea only outwardly arrayed the kingdom of matter and of death with the veil of the beauty of nature. It had to enter this kingdom *from within*, through humanity and the action of its universal rational consciousness, in order to enliven nature anew and make its beauty immortal. In this sense it is necessary to change the relation of the human being to nature. He must establish with her that syzygetic unity, by which his true life in the personal and communal spheres is determined.

V

Nature has hitherto been either the all-powerful, despotic mother of an infant humanity, or a slave alien to it, a thing. In this second epoch the poets alone have still preserved, at least upheld, an unaccountable and timid feeling of love towards nature, as towards a being enjoying equal rights and possessing, or capable of possessing, *life in itself.* The true poets have always remained the prophets of the worldwide rehabilitation of life and of beauty. As one of them has well said to his fellows:

> Only with you as with friends of old
> Are fleeting day dreams mirrored in the soul,
> Only with you do the fragrant roses
> Glisten for ever with tears of rapture.
> From earthly markets, hueless and stifling,
> What joy to behold the delicate tints
> In your transparent aerial rainbows.
> To me they seem blessings from a native heaven.[6]

The establishment of a true loving or syzygetic relation in humanity with not only its social, but also its natural and cosmic environment—this end in itself is plain. It is not possible to say the same about the paths of its attainment by the individual human being. Without going into premature and therefore questionable and untimely details, it is possible, basing oneself upon solid analogies of cosmic and historical experience, to assert with firm confidence that any conscious activity of humanity determined by the idea of a cosmic syzygy

116

and aimed at embodying the unity-of-the-all ideal in that sphere or another actually produces or sets free real currents of spirit and body. These currents gradually take possession of the material environment, animate it and embody in it some images or other of the unity-of-the-all—the living and eternal likenesses of absolute humanity. The power of this spiritual-corporeal creativeness in human beings is only a transformation or *directing inward* of that same creative power which in nature, being directed outward, produces the basic infinity of physical propagation of organisms.

Having in the idea of a worldwide syzygy connected (individual sexual) love with the true essence of universal life, I have accomplished my immediate task—to specify the meaning of love; seeing that by the meaning of any object whatsoever is understood its very internal bond with universal truth. So far as certain specialized questions which I have been obliged to touch upon are concerned, I propose to turn to them again.

1. [Source not identified.]

2. [From a poem by the Russian poet, Fet, the pen name of A. A. Shenshin (1820–1892).]

3. [The philosopher's stone was a substance capable of transforming the baser metals into gold or silver.]

117

4. [Sir Isaac Newton (1642–1727) in the queries to his work *Optics* identifies space as the *sensorium* of God.]

5. From the Greek συζυγια—close union. I am compelled to introduce this neologism since I cannot discover in the existent terminology any other and better one. I note that the Gnostics used the word συζυγια in another meaning, and that, in general, the use by heretics of a certain term still does not make it heretical.

6. [Fet.]